ISBN: 979-8-9963307-0-6 (Paperback)
ISBN: 979-8-9963307-1-3 (eBook)

Published by Steadfast Resources, Ltd. Co.

steadfastltd.io

To God, whose grace held what we could not carry,
and whose redemption has made nothing wasted.

To Silvia, my bride,
who walked every hard mile of this journey beside me.

To my three remarkable children,
who paid a price they did not choose
and have become people worthy of every cost.

And to every family carrying more than they know how to say.

May God be glorified in every page,
and may you find in these words
what we wish someone had placed in our hands.

Table of Contents

Foreword: What I Didn't See iii

Introduction xii

1. Adapting Your Approach: Communication Across Different Personalities and Styles 1
2. Understanding Today's Children and Young Adults (10-24) 8
3. 3rd Culture Kids: Their Unique Struggle is Real 21
4. Warning Signs: Identifying At-Risk Behaviors 52
5. Biblical Understanding: The Heart Behind Behavior 64
6. Approaching Difficult Conversations 79
7. Biblical Intervention Strategies 87
8. Digital Life, Substances, and At-Risk Behaviors 98
9. Faith, Identity, and Sexuality 106
10. Self-Harm: Understanding and Responding with Biblical Wisdom .. 116
11. Suicide Intervention: A Life-Saving Guide for Parents 133
12. Nurturing Your Relationship Through Challenges 152
13. Prayer Guide for Parents 161
14. Conclusion: The Long View of Parenting 170

Foreword: What I Didn't See

A Personal Word from the Author

I did not write this book from a distance. I wrote it from the inside of the story it describes, as a father who loved his children deeply, who was present in their lives every day, and who still managed to miss what was happening right in front of him. That is not a story unique to internationally mobile families. It is the story of parenthood itself. The specific geography of my family's journey was cross-cultural ministry. But the blindness I carried, the grief I discovered too late, and the grace that has held me since, those belong to every parent who has ever wondered whether they saw their child clearly enough when it mattered most.

My wife and I went to serve. We believed we were called. And we were. I do not doubt that now any more than I doubted it then. We saw lives transformed. We saw people whom society had discarded find dignity, hope, and redemption in the love of Christ. We were given the extraordinary privilege of witnessing God's mercy and grace in ways that most people never see in a lifetime. That is all true, and I would not trade it.

But there is another truth that took me years to face, and it is the reason this resource exists: I was ill-equipped to protect my children. And while I was watching God transform the lives of others, I was missing what was happening in the lives of the three people sleeping under my own roof. I share this not because our story is exceptional, but because I have come to believe it is far more common than any of us want to admit, in ministry families and military families, in homes abroad and homes right here, in families that love God and love their children and still find themselves looking back with grief at what they did not see in time.

The First Day

I remember the day my son came home from his first day at his new school. He was ten years old. I expected the usual adjustment; nerves, unfamiliarity, the ordinary awkwardness of being new. What he told me instead stopped me cold.

Many of the girls in the school had surrounded him. They wanted to touch him; his hair, his skin, his arms, because he looked so different from everyone they had ever known. He was ten years old, and he felt violated. He hated it. He came home and told us, in the plain words of a ten-year-old, that he hated his new school.

We told him it was because he was new. We told him it would stop soon enough.

It didn't stop. It went on for years. The girls continued. The boys, resenting the attention the girls gave him, turned against him in their own way. He was targeted from both sides, and he carried it silently because he knew, the way children always know, that we needed him to be okay. He never told us just how bad it had become. Not until he was much older. Not until the foreign ministry years were behind us and we were sitting together in the safety of hindsight.

When I finally understood the full weight of what he had endured and understood that I had seen the beginning of it on that very first day and chosen reassurance over action; I felt, and I still feel, that I had failed to protect my son. That is not a feeling that goes away easily. It is something a father carries always.

> "*He heals the brokenhearted and binds up their wounds.*" - Psalm 147:3

The Child Between Two Languages

My middle child lost her identity somewhere between two continents and two languages. Her first spoken language was English, while her first reading language was Spanish. By the time we repatriated to the United States, she had very few memories of ever having lived there. America, her passport country, the place she was supposed to belong, felt as foreign to her as any country we had ever been posted to.

She struggled more than any of our children during repatriation. Making friends was hard. Adapting to a culture she was supposed to already know was hard. She was caught between worlds in the way that only a child who has grown up across languages and borders can truly understand, belonging fully to neither, carrying pieces of both, uncertain of where to plant her feet. She told me as a pre-teen at the time that she felt like the kids here live in a bubble and have no idea that it is a big and dangerous world. I saw that she could not relate to those around her and they could not relate to her. Her view of the world was so big, and the kids here could not understand it.

I wish I had known then what I know now about what repatriation actually costs a child who has never truly lived in their passport country. I wish I had known that coming home is not always a homecoming. For my daughter, it was another move to a foreign country, except this time, no one acknowledged it as such.

The One Who Never Knew Another Home

My youngest was two years old when we left the U.S. She was three when we moved to Colombia, South America. She had no memories of the United States at all, no frame of reference for the country she was eventually supposed to return to, no sense that anything had been left behind, because she had never been old enough to know it.

What we did not anticipate was how much she was already carrying, even then, even at four years old in a world that was not yet hers in any language.

We had a rule in our home, in Mexico and again in Colombia: Spanish outside the house, English inside. She arrived in Colombia just weeks before her fourth birthday with almost no Spanish at all. We enrolled her in the same school her siblings attended, believing she would find her footing once friendships began to form. Children adapt, we told ourselves. She would find her way.

A couple of months in, we received a call from her teacher. She asked careful, probing questions. Was our daughter struggling with learning? Did she have difficulty speaking? We were genuinely confused. At home, she was relentlessly talkative, the kind of child who narrated everything she saw and questioned everything she did not yet understand. We told the teacher so. The teacher listened, and then told us what she had actually been observing: a small girl sitting silently at the back of the room, never volunteering, never responding, keeping entirely to herself.

We asked her about it that evening. She said school was fine, but that the other kids were not very nice. The teacher, though, she liked the teacher. She liked going. It was the only answer a four-year-old could give, because the weight of what she was navigating was not something she had words for yet, in any language. The most we could determine was that the language barrier had become a wall she did not yet know how to cross. So she sat behind it, and she listened.

About six months in, we received a second call from the school. This one was different.

Out of the blue, our daughter had begun speaking in class. Not haltingly, not with the careful stumbling of a child still acquiring a language, but fluently, in near-perfect Spanish. The entire time she had been sitting quietly at the back of the room, she had been learning. She had been watching every face, absorbing every sound, building a language inside herself that no one around her knew she possessed. She had simply waited until she was ready.

She made a friend, and then the teacher had an entirely different problem: she would not stop talking during class.

There is a moment I will always remember, recounted to us by the teacher with equal parts exasperation and amusement. Our daughter had asked to use the restroom and was apparently discovered playing in the water, a charge she has denied emphatically ever since, and continues to deny with considerable conviction. The consequence was the corner. The consequence, in her estimation, was unjust. And so when the lesson came to a review of animal names and colors, and the teacher called on her, she answered every question in English. Every single one. Perfect, deliberate, unhurried English, addressed to a teacher who did not speak a word of it. She knew every animal. She knew every color. She knew them in both languages without any difficulty at all. She simply chose, on that particular morning, not to demonstrate that in Spanish.

I did not know, in that moment, whether to discipline her or to be quietly proud of her. I was, in truth, both.

She reached a point, in the months that followed, where she could move between her two languages the way a river moves between banks, mid-sentence, without pause, without effort, as if the line between them simply did not exist for her. She was, and is, a remarkable person.

But Colombia was not without its shadows for her. As she grew older within that community, the social pressures surrounding her became harder to navigate. Children in her peer group were being pressed by each other, and by a kind of cultural current none of them were old enough to name, toward romantic relationships no child that age was ready for. Boys pursued her attention in ways that were completely inappropriate. It reminded us, sharply, that vulnerability in any cultural context does not wait until a child is old enough to understand it.

She carried all of that, more than any child should have to carry. And for far too long, we did not fully see it.

The Cost I Did Not Count

When Jesus spoke about counting the cost before building a tower (Luke 14:28), I understood that verse as a call to commitment and organization. I counted the cost of ministry. I counted the sacrifice of leaving home, of financial uncertainty, of cultural distance, of the difficulty and danger that cross-cultural work sometimes involves. I counted all of it and said yes.

What I did not count, what I did not know how to count, was what it would cost my children. Not because I did not love them. I loved them with everything I had. But I did not have the tools, the awareness, or the resources to understand what growing up across cultures, languages, and countries was doing to them beneath the surface. I did not know what to watch for. I did not know the questions to ask. I did not know that my son's first-day report was the beginning of something I needed to take seriously immediately.

The moment I finally understood the full weight of what my children had carried, each of them, in their own way, the hurt was almost more than I could bear. If it were not for God's grace and mercy, I do not know how I would carry it even now.

> *"My grace is sufficient for you, for my power is made perfect in weakness."* - 2 Corinthians 12:9

What God Did With It

I need to tell you something else, because this foreword cannot end in grief alone. That would not be honest either.

My son, the boy who came home from his first day of school at ten years old and told me he hated it, the young man who carried years of isolation and targeting in silence, is a faithful, God-loving adult. He has told me that he does not blame us for what happened. He has told me that he knows God used those years to form the person he is today, and that he gives God all the glory for it. Those words, spoken freely and without obligation, are among the most grace-filled things I have ever heard.

My daughters, who are the most incredible people I know and whom I admire more than they know, but who have suffered so greatly, have triumphed over insurmountable challenges that most girls would never have to face. God has formed and shaped them into strong, independent, Godly women who love Jesus. In their own unique ways, they have shown us unwarranted clemency, forgiveness and grace.

I do not share that to resolve the grief too quickly or to suggest that the wounds were not real. They were real. They mattered. They still matter. But I share it because it is true, and because the parent reading this foreword at their lowest moment, wondering if they have already missed something irreparable in their child, needs to know that God's redemptive reach is longer than our failures.

Romans 8:28 is not a greeting card verse. It is a promise that has been tested in my family, across multiple countries, in the lives of three children who paid a price they did not choose, and it has held. What the enemy intended as a deep wound, God has used as formation. I have seen it with my own eyes, in my own children.

> "*And we know that for those who love God all things work together for good, for those who are called according to his purpose.*" (Romans 8:28)

Why This Resource Exists

STEADFAST exists because I did not have it. My wife and I navigated the international parenting years without a roadmap for what our children were experiencing, without language for what we were seeing, and without a biblically grounded framework for responding to the specific challenges that cross-cultural family life generates. We loved God. We loved our children. My wife and I spent four years in cross-cultural ministry in Mexico and Colombia, and it was in those years, watching God transform the lives of others while missing what was happening in the lives of our own children, that the need for this resource became undeniable. We were not enough, on our own, to bridge the gap between those two things and what our children actually needed.

This resource is my attempt to give the next generation of parents what I wish someone had placed in my hands. It is not written from a place of having done it perfectly. It is written from a place of having done it imperfectly, of having grieved what that cost, of having watched God redeem what I could not fix, and of believing that the families reading this deserve better tools than the ones that were available to us.

Every section of this resource was written with specific children in mind, children like my son, who suffered in silence because he didn't want to burden us. Children like my daughter, who lost her footing between two worlds. Children like my youngest, who carried more than she should have and never let us see it. But also children who have never left their hometown, who are struggling to belong, to believe, to find their way through adolescence in a world that is more complex and more dangerous than the one their parents grew up in. The heart behind every chapter is the same regardless of the geography: a parent who loves their child and needs better tools to see them clearly.

If you are reading this as a parent who is already in the international years, I want you to know: it is not too late. The awareness you are building right now, in this moment, is the gift you can give your child today. You do not need to have seen everything you should have seen. You need to start seeing now.

If you are reading this as a parent who has come home, who is sitting in the repatriation years wondering why your child is struggling in a country they are supposed to belong to, I want you to know: what you are seeing is real, it has a name, and there is a way through it.

If you are reading this as a parent whose family has never lived abroad, whose child is struggling with identity, belonging, faith, or any of the quiet crises that adolescence carries regardless of where a family has lived, this resource was written for you too. The tools here are grounded in Scripture and in the unchanging nature of what children need from their parents. The geography changes. Those needs do not.

You were not meant to carry this alone. This resource was written to give you a framework, but a framework is not a community. That is why, alongside this book, we built WayFinder, a community for families navigating exactly what these pages describe, where cross-cultural parents, missionary families, and those walking through the challenges of raising children in a complex world can find one another, learn together, and be known. The book you hold is a starting point. You can take the next step at steadfastltd.io.

And if you are reading this as a parent who is looking back, as I have looked back, carrying the weight of what you did not see in time, I want you to know that I am writing this from exactly that place. You are not alone in it. And the God who was present in every hard season, every school, every goodbye, every ordinary Tuesday when your child was struggling and you did not yet know it, He has not finished the work He began in them. He who began a good work will carry it on to completion.

> "*He who began a good work in you will carry it on to completion until the day of Christ Jesus.*" -Philippians 1:6

Jeff Roddy
CEO, Steadfast Resources, Ltd. Co.
Austin, Texas USA
2026

Introduction

What is STEADFAST?

STEADFAST is a comprehensive, Bible-based toolkit designed to help parents navigate the challenges of raising children and young adults in today's complex world. Published by Steadfast Resources, Ltd. Co., this resource provides practical guidance, biblical wisdom, and evidence-based strategies for parents of young people ages 10-24.

At its core, STEADFAST equips parents to:

- Recognize warning signs of at-risk behaviors
- Understand the heart issues behind concerning behaviors
- Approach difficult conversations with wisdom and grace
- Implement effective, age-appropriate intervention strategies
- Support their children's spiritual, emotional, and mental wellbeing
- Know when and how to seek additional help when needed

This resource is not simply a parenting manual, it is a compass that points to God's unchanging truth while addressing very real challenges facing families today, including digital pressures, mental health concerns, identity formation, and spiritual development.

Dear Parents,

The journey from childhood through adolescence and into young adulthood encompasses critical seasons of development, challenge, and spiritual formation. As parents of young people between 10-24, you walk alongside them through tremendous physical, emotional, social, and spiritual changes. Your role evolves during these years, but your influence and guidance remain essential at every stage.

Steadfast Resources has developed this resource to address the unique challenges faced by parents of preteens, teenagers, and young adults in today's complex world. The widening of our focus to include children as young as 10 reflects the reality that many challenges, including mental health concerns, digital pressures, and identity formation, are now affecting children at younger ages than in previous generations.

Since returning to the United States in 2014 and founding the Seekers International Foundation, we have spent more than a decade walking alongside families navigating exactly these challenges, across the United States and throughout South America, including Colombia, Brazil, Argentina, and Peru. We have conducted suicide intervention workshops with parents and youth workers in communities across the country. We have sat with families in crisis and with families trying to get ahead of one. What we have learned from that work, alongside everything we learned the hard way in our own family, is what shaped every chapter of this resource.

We want to encourage you: Don't give up, even when parenting feels overwhelming. When you face resistance, setbacks, or feel inadequate to the task, remember that God has specifically chosen you for this sacred calling of raising your child. As Hebrews 12:1 reminds us, "Let us run with perseverance the race marked out for us." Your consistent efforts, guided by biblical wisdom and bathed in prayer, will bear fruit, even when progress seems slow, invisible and impossible.

We urge you to follow the recommendations in this resource to the best of your ability, not as a rigid formula but as a flexible framework that can be adapted to your family's unique needs. No parent implements every strategy perfectly, but your willingness to learn, grow, and persevere makes a profound difference in your child's life. Remember that you're not alone on this journey, God walks with you, and the community of believers stands ready to support you as you raise your children in the way they should go.

How to Use This Resource

STEADFAST is designed to be flexible, allowing you to engage with it in multiple ways based on your specific needs:

1. **As a Complete Guidebook**
   Read through the entire resource from beginning to end to gain a comprehensive understanding of biblically grounded parenting across all developmental stages. This approach provides the fullest context and allows you to see how various concepts connect.

2. **As a Targeted Reference**
   Use the detailed Table of Contents to quickly locate specific topics relevant to your current parenting challenges. Each section stands alone while still connecting to the broader framework.

3. **As a Development-Stage Guide**
   Focus on the age range most relevant to your child:
   - For parents of pre-teens (10-13): Pay special attention to Sections 1-4
   - For parents of teenagers (14-17): Concentrate on Sections 2-7
   - For parents of young adults (18-24): Emphasize Sections 5-11

4. **As a Crisis Resource**
   In urgent situations, jump directly to Sections 10-11 (Self-Harm and Suicide Intervention) or use the "When to Seek Additional Help" guidance in Section 7.

5. **As a Small Group Study**
   Form a group with other parents to work through STEADFAST together, using each chapter as a starting point for conversation and mutual support. A companion workbook with structured discussion questions and practical exercises for each chapter is currently in development through Steadfast Resources.

Implementation Tips:

1. **Start with Prayer**
   Before engaging with any section, pray for wisdom and discernment in applying these principles to your specific family context.

2. **Take Notes**
   Keep a journal alongside this resource to record insights, questions, and specific applications for your family.

3. **Involve Your Spouse/Co-parent**
   If possible, work through this material together with your child's other parent or guardians to ensure consistency.

4. **Be Patient with the Process**
   Lasting change takes time. Focus on progress rather than perfection as you implement these principles.

5. **Personalize the Content**
   Every family and every child is unique. Adapt these strategies to fit your child's personality, strengths, and challenges.

6. **Revisit Regularly**
   As your child grows and circumstances change, different sections will become more relevant. Return to this resource regularly throughout your parenting journey.

> ✈ **FROM THE FIELD**
>
> *Our oldest daughter was being bullied in Colombia, mocked in Spanish she didn't yet understand, her things stolen, names called, the girls in her class systematically unkind. She never told us. Instead, she handled it the only way available to her: she fought back. We were called into the school office more than once because she had gotten into a physical altercation with girls and boys who were targeting her.*
>
> *We disciplined her for fighting. We talked to her about better ways to handle conflict. What we did not know, what we did not find out until later, was that she had also quietly appointed herself the protector of the smaller children in her class and others who couldn't protect themselves. And she was doing the same thing for her brother and sister at home.*
>
> *She was communicating the entire time. She just wasn't using words. Children who cannot tell you what is happening will almost always show you instead: in their behavior, their choices, the things they take into their own hands. The question is whether we are paying attention to the right things.*

When Children Don't Open Up

One of the most significant challenges parents face is that children and young adults often struggle to communicate openly about their problems. This reluctance to share can stem from various sources:

- Fear of disappointing parents or facing judgment
- Desire for independence and to solve problems on their own
- Uncertainty about how to express complex feelings
- Concerns about parental reactions or overreactions
- Loyalty to peers and fear of "telling on" friends

- Embarrassment or shame about their struggles
- Previous negative experiences when sharing difficult information

When faced with a child who isn't communicating openly, consider these approaches:

1. **Create Alternative Communication Channels**: Some young people communicate better through writing than talking. Consider establishing a journal that you both write in, exchanging letters, or even texting serious conversations if that creates a safer space for your child.

2. **Enlist Trusted Adults**: Sometimes teens will open up to other adults when they won't talk to parents. Cultivate relationships with youth leaders, coaches, aunts/uncles, or family friends who share your values and can serve as additional listening ears.

3. **Watch for Indirect Communication**: Pay attention to what your child communicates indirectly, through music choices, art, social media posts, or conversations with siblings. These often provide windows into their inner world.

4. **Focus on Emotional Safety**: Evaluate your typical responses. If you tend to lecture, problem-solve immediately, or display strong emotional reactions, your child may stay silent to avoid these responses. Practice calm listening without immediate solutions.

5. **Seek Professional Support**: When concerns persist despite your best efforts, consider professional help. Counselors and therapists are trained to create spaces where young people feel safe discussing difficult topics.

6. **Engage Through Activities**: Side-by-side activities often create natural spaces for conversation. Car rides, walking, cooking, or

engaging in a shared hobby can lead to more open communication than face-to-face questioning.

Remember that your child's reluctance to open up is typically not a reflection of their relationship with you but rather a normal developmental step toward independence or a protective mechanism. With patience, wisdom, and the right approaches, you can create pathways for honest communication even during challenging seasons.

This resource is designed to help you:

- Identify potential warning signs of at-risk behaviors across different developmental stages
- Understand the underlying causes from a biblical perspective
- Approach difficult conversations with wisdom and grace appropriate to your child's age
- Implement biblical strategies for healthy intervention
- Support your child's journey toward spiritual maturity
- Recognize when and how to seek professional help

Throughout this journey, remember that God's Word provides timeless wisdom for every challenge:

"*Start children off on the way they should go, and even when they are old they will not turn from it.*" (Proverbs 22:6)

"*I have no greater joy than to hear that my children are walking in the truth.*" (3 John 1:4)

1. Adapting Your Approach: Communication Across Different Personalities and Styles

Different children respond to different communication approaches, particularly based on their personality type and natural communication style. Understanding these differences can help you connect more effectively with your child.

Introverted vs. Extroverted Children

Communicating with Introverted Children:

- **Give Processing Time**: Introverted children often need time to process their thoughts before responding. Allow for comfortable silences without pressure.
- **Provide Advance Notice**: When possible, let them know ahead of time that you want to discuss something important, giving them time to prepare mentally.
- **Use Written Communication**: Many introverts express themselves more comfortably in writing. Consider a shared journal, text messages, or notes for deeper topics.
- **One-on-One Settings**: Introverts typically open up more in private conversations without siblings or other family members present.
- **Respect Energy Limits**: Be mindful that extended conversations can be draining for introverts. Watch for signs of fatigue and be willing to continue the conversation later.

- **Side-by-Side Activities**: Many introverted children talk more freely while engaged in an activity (driving, walking, cooking) rather than in face-to-face conversations.

Communicating with Extroverted Children:

- **Active Engagement**: Extroverted children often think while talking, so they may need more interactive dialogue to process their thoughts.
- **Group Discussion Options**: Some extroverts may benefit from family discussions where multiple perspectives help them clarify their thinking.
- **Physical Movement**: Many extroverted children communicate better when they can move around rather than sitting still for a serious talk.
- **Verbal Processing Time**: Allow them to talk through their ideas, even if initial thoughts seem off-topic or rambling.
- **Enthusiastic Response**: Extroverts often draw energy from engaged facial expressions and verbal affirmations during conversation.
- **Activity-Based Talks**: Combining conversations with engaging activities can keep energetic extroverts focused on the discussion.

Male vs. Female Communication Patterns

While individual differences are significant and stereotypes should be avoided, research shows some general tendencies in male and female communication styles that may be helpful to consider:

Communication with Sons:

- **Solution-Focused Approach**: Many boys respond well to conversations that address problems directly and explore potential solutions.
- **Information Orientation**: Communication that provides clear information without requiring immediate emotional processing often works well.
- **Action Language**: Frame discussions around actions and choices rather than feelings and experiences.
- **Shoulder-to-Shoulder**: Boys often open up more during shared activities rather than direct face-to-face conversations.
- **Respecting Silence**: Many boys process internally and may need space before articulating thoughts, especially about emotional topics.
- **Direct Questions**: Specific, concrete questions often work better than general "how do you feel" inquiries with many boys.

Communication with Daughters:

- **Relational Focus**: Many girls respond well to conversations that acknowledge the impact of issues on relationships.
- **Emotional Validation**: Taking time to acknowledge and validate feelings before moving to solutions is often important.
- **Active Listening Cues**: Visual and verbal signals that you're listening and understanding her perspective encourage further sharing.
- **Face-to-Face Connection**: Direct eye contact and focused attention may facilitate openness for many girls.

- **Detail Opportunity**: Creating space for sharing details and context rather than just the main points can lead to deeper conversations.
- **Narrative Approach**: Framing discussions within stories or personal experiences may resonate more strongly.

Adapting For Your Child's Unique Style

Remember that these are general patterns, not rigid rules. Your child is unique and may communicate in ways that don't align with typical patterns for their gender or apparent personality type. The key is observation and adaptation:

1. **Observe When They Open Up**: Notice the circumstances when your child naturally shares more. What time of day, setting, or approach seems to work?
2. **Ask Directly**: For older children and teens, consider asking: "How do you prefer we talk about important things? When and how would these conversations be most comfortable for you?"
3. **Experiment**: Try different approaches based on your observations and their feedback, noticing which seem most effective.
4. **Respect Their Style**: Rather than forcing your preferred communication style, adapt to theirs when possible, especially for important conversations.
5. **Balance Challenge and Comfort**: Sometimes stretching beyond comfort zones is necessary, but build primarily on communication strengths.
6. **Pray For Wisdom**: Ask God for discernment to understand and connect with your child's unique communication style.

The goal is not to label children but to honor their God-given uniqueness and find the most effective ways to maintain open communication about important matters, especially when addressing concerns about at-risk behaviors.

✈ FROM THE FIELD

No two of my three children were alike in the way they needed to be reached, and raising them internationally, where everything else was already in constant flux, made learning each of them both more urgent and more difficult than it might have been in a stable environment.

My son needed facts and directness. He is analytical by nature, and emotional language felt like interference to him. What communicated love and respect to him was clear, honest information delivered without excess. My middle daughter needed the opposite: emotional validation always came first, before any content could land. She needed to know she was felt, before she could hear anything I was trying to say. My youngest needed something different still: genuine presence, face-to-face, active listening without agenda. She would open up, but only when she was certain she had my full and unhurried attention.

I did not arrive at this understanding quickly or gracefully. I got it wrong with each of them before I began to get it right. But the learning itself, slow and humbling as it was, became one of the most important things I did as their father. Every parent must learn their child's language. The question is only how long we wait before we start.

Words of Encouragement:

There is a particular kind of grief that does not get much attention in parenting conversations. It is the grief of realizing, sometimes years in, that the way you have been trying to reach your child has not been working. Not because you did not love them. Not because you did not try. But because you were speaking your language, not theirs, and no one told you that your languages were different. Scripture acknowledges the depth of what is hidden inside a person: "The purposes of a person's heart are deep waters, but one who has insight draws them out" (Proverbs 20:5). Your child's inner world runs deep. Drawing it out requires the kind of patient, attentive love that learns to ask better questions before it reaches for answers.

If this chapter has surfaced that realization for you, sit with it honestly. It is not a comfortable thing to recognize. But consider what it means that you are recognizing it at all. A parent who does not love their child deeply does not feel the weight of that discovery. The weight itself is evidence of the love. Scripture describes love as something that "bears all things, believes all things, hopes all things, endures all things" (1 Corinthians 13:7). The endurance love calls for is not passive. It is the active, ongoing commitment to keep trying, keep learning, keep showing up, even after previous attempts have fallen short. The question now is not how to undo the past. It is what you do with what you know today.

Learning to speak a new language as an adult is harder than learning it as a child. The same is true of communication. If you have spent years approaching your child one way, shifting that approach requires deliberate effort, and it will feel awkward at first. You will get it wrong some days. Your child may not immediately respond to the change, or may even be suspicious of it. That is normal. James offers a seemingly simple framework for this work: "Let every person be quick to hear, slow to speak, slow to anger" (James 1:19). Quick to hear is first. Before the new words, there must be genuine listening, the kind that is not planning its response while the other person is still talking. Trust is rebuilt slowly, through that kind of consistent, unhurried attention.

What Scripture offers here is not a technique. It is a model. Jesus, speaking to fishermen, spoke of nets and fish and the sea (Matthew 4:19). Speaking to a farmer, he spoke of seeds and soil and harvest (Mark 4:3-9). Speaking to a woman at a well, he spoke of living water (John 4:10-14). He went to where people already were and spoke in a language they already understood. He did not ask them to meet him on his terms before he would engage with theirs. That is not compromise. That is love taking the shape of the person it is trying to reach, and it is the model this chapter is placing in your hands.

You are not being asked to become a different parent. You are being asked to become a more attentive one, to study your child the way you would study a language you genuinely want to learn, not because you have to but because the person on the other side of that language is worth understanding. God Himself models this attentiveness. "You have searched me, Lord, and you know me. You know when I sit and when I rise; you perceive my thoughts from afar" (Psalm 139:1-2). The God who made your child knows them that completely. That kind of knowing, patient and specific and deeply personal, is what you are being invited to pursue in your own relationship with them.

When communication still feels difficult, when you try the new approach and it does not seem to land, hold onto this: the Holy Spirit is not limited by your imperfect attempts. "The Spirit helps us in our weakness. We do not know what we ought to pray for, but the Spirit himself intercedes for us through wordless groans" (Romans 8:26). If the Spirit intercedes in the moments when we do not even have the words to pray, He is certainly at work in the imperfect, halting attempts of a parent trying to reach their child. You are not the only one pursuing your child. God is pursuing them too, with a love and a fluency that surpasses anything you could offer on your own. Trust that partnership. Keep showing up. The investment you are making in learning to truly know your child will yield fruit, in His time, in ways you cannot yet measure.

2. Understanding Today's Children and Young Adults (10-24)

The Unique Challenges They Face

Young people ages 10-24 navigate challenges that vary by developmental stage but share common themes:

Pre-teens and Early Adolescents (10-13)

- **Initial Identity Questions**: Beginning to question "who am I?" while still largely influenced by family
- **Social Awakening**: Increased awareness of peer relationships and social dynamics
- **Digital Introduction**: Often receiving first smartphones and social media exposure
- **Bodily Changes**: Navigating the early physical and emotional changes of puberty
- **Spiritual Questioning**: Moving from inherited faith toward more personal understanding

Middle Adolescents (14-17)

- **Identity Experimentation**: Trying on different identities and peer groups
- **Digital Immersion**: Deeper engagement with social media and online culture
- **Academic Pressure**: Increasing school demands and future-oriented decisions
- **Risk Behaviors**: Potential exposure to substances, sexual activity, and other adult behaviors
- **Authority Questioning**: Testing boundaries with parents and other authority figures

Late Adolescents and Young Adults (18-24)

- **Identity Consolidation**: Solidifying sense of self and life direction
- **Digital Dependency**: Managing technology use in increasingly independent settings
- **Major Life Transitions**: Educational decisions, career exploration, relationship formation
- **Worldview Solidification**: Determining personal values and beliefs among competing options
- **Delayed Independence**: Many young adults taking longer to achieve traditional markers of adulthood

Challenges Across All Ages

- **Digital Pressures**: Constant comparison on social media and unprecedented access to harmful content
- **Mental Health Vulnerabilities**: Rising rates of anxiety, depression, and isolation beginning at younger ages
- **Worldview Confusion**: Exposure to conflicting belief systems and values
- **Diminished Face-to-Face Connection**: Reduced in-person social skills and community engagement
- **Accelerated Exposure**: Earlier access to adult content, issues, and decisions

The Adolescent Brain: Why Behavior Makes Sense

One of the most important things a parent of a child between the ages of 10 and 24 can understand is that the brain itself is in a period of profound development. The prefrontal cortex, the region responsible for decision-making, impulse control, emotional regulation, and long-term thinking, is not fully developed until the mid-twenties. This is not a character flaw or a spiritual failure. It is biology.

What this means practically is that adolescents are neurologically wired to seek sensation, respond emotionally before thinking rationally, underestimate consequences, and prioritize peer connection over parental guidance. These tendencies are frustrating to navigate and can produce genuinely risky behavior, but they are also a normal part of how God designed the maturing human brain.

For families navigating significant life transitions, whether across cultures or across circumstances, this developmental reality can intersect with an additional layer of pressure. The emotional regulation challenges of adolescence are amplified when a young person is also managing change, loss, displacement, or instability. A brain that is already struggling to regulate emotion is being asked to do so under conditions that would challenge even a fully developed adult. Understanding this does not excuse behavior. It helps parents respond with the wisdom the moment requires rather than the frustration it provokes.

A note on family composition: The challenges described throughout this chapter apply across a wide range of family structures. Adoptive families navigating questions of identity and belonging will find much of this material directly relevant. Families navigating extended separations for any reason, whether due to work, ministry, illness, or circumstance, face a specific form of relational wound that deserves acknowledgment. The prolonged physical absence of one or both parents creates an attachment burden that compounds the developmental challenges described here. If your family's structure differs from the traditional two-parent household, know that this resource was written with you in mind as well.

> **✈ FROM THE FIELD**
>
> *When we repatriated to the United States, my middle daughter was a pre-teen trying to find her footing in a culture she was supposed to already know. She had grown up speaking English and reading Spanish, carrying two worlds inside her, and she could not understand why the children around her seemed so unbothered by everything.*
>
> *She said something to me once that I have never forgotten. She said that the kids here live in a bubble and have no idea that it is a big and dangerous world.*
>
> *She was not wrong. She had lived in countries where that danger was visible and close. Her view of the world was simply larger, and that largeness made her feel more foreign in her own passport country than she had ever felt abroad. Understanding your child begins with understanding the world they are actually carrying inside them, whether or not that world is visible to anyone else.*

A note on depression and irritability: Parents often expect a depressed teenager to appear sad. In adolescents, depression frequently presents as irritability, moodiness, anger, or unexplained physical complaints. A teenager who seems consistently frustrated, reactive, or emotionally volatile may not simply be going through a difficult phase. They may be experiencing a clinical condition that responds to professional support. Withdrawal is not always grief. Sometimes it is depression, and the two require different responses.

What Biblical Identity Looks Like

The foundation of healthy development is understanding one's identity in Christ. This theological framework provides stability amidst the identity confusion so prevalent in adolescent and young adult development.

1. **Created by Design, Not by Accident**

   Scripture teaches that each young person is intentionally crafted by God:

   "*For you created my inmost being; you knit me together in my mother's womb. I praise you because I am fearfully and wonderfully made; your works are wonderful, I know that full well.*" (Psalm 139:13-14)

   The doctrine of divine creation means:

   - Each young person exists because God specifically willed them into being
   - Their physical traits, personality, and gifts reflect God's intentional craftsmanship
   - Their existence has inherent purpose, regardless of the circumstances of their conception or birth
   - They bear the divine image (imago Dei) as image-bearers of God Himself (Genesis 1:27)
   - Their bodies are not accidental collections of cells but divinely designed temples (1 Corinthians 6:19-20)

   This contrasts sharply with secular narratives of random existence or being merely the product of biological processes.

2. **Intrinsically Valuable, Not Comparatively Valuable**

   In God's economy, worth is inherent, not earned or comparative:

   > "*Are not five sparrows sold for two pennies? Yet not one of them is forgotten by God. Indeed, the very hairs of your head*

> *are all numbered. Don't be afraid; you are worth more than many sparrows."* (Luke 12:6-7)

> *"For God so loved the world that he gave his one and only Son, that whoever believes in him shall not perish but have eternal life."* (John 3:16)

This biblical understanding of value means:

- A young person's worth is established by God's love, not social media metrics
- Their value doesn't fluctuate based on achievements, appearance, or social acceptance
- They are worth the incalculable price of Christ's sacrifice
- They have dignity that transcends their utility, productivity, or status
- No failure or rejection can diminish their fundamental worth to God

This provides a crucial anchor against the comparative value system of social media and peer culture.

3. Defined by Relationship with God, Not Performance

Biblical identity centers on relationship rather than achievement:

> *"Yet to all who did receive him, to those who believed in his name, he gave the right to become children of God, children born not of natural descent, nor of human decision or a husband's will, but born of God."* (John 1:12-13)

> *"The Spirit you received does not make you slaves, so that you live in fear again; rather, the Spirit you received brought about your adoption to sonship. And by him we cry, 'Abba,*

Father.' The Spirit himself testifies with our spirit that we are God's children." (Romans 8:15-16)

The theological reality of adoption means:

- Young people find their primary identity as beloved children of God
- Their relationship with God is not based on religious performance or moral perfection
- They have the privilege of intimate access to the Father (Galatians 4:6-7)
- Their identity is secured by legal adoption into God's family, not by feeling close to God
- They are co-heirs with Christ, with all the rights and privileges of true children (Romans 8:17)

This relational identity provides a stable alternative to performance-based identities that dominate academic, athletic, and social spheres.

4. Redeemed and Forgiven, Not Defined by Past Mistakes

The gospel assures young people that their mistakes don't determine their identity:

> *"Therefore, if anyone is in Christ, the new creation has come: The old has gone, the new is here!"* (2 Corinthians 5:17)
>
> *"As far as the east is from the west, so far has he removed our transgressions from us."* (Psalm 103:12)

This redemptive identity means:

- Young people are not defined by their worst moments or biggest mistakes

- Their identity is not determined by their success or failure at resisting temptation
- They can experience genuine transformation through Christ's work
- Their past does not dictate their future in God's economy
- They are being progressively conformed to Christ's image (Romans 8:29; 2 Corinthians 3:18)

This provides hope and a fresh start for adolescents navigating the consequences of poor choices.

5. Called to Purpose in God's Kingdom

Biblical identity includes participation in God's redemptive mission:

> "*For we are God's handiwork, created in Christ Jesus to do good works, which God prepared in advance for us to do.*" (Ephesians 2:10)

> "*But you are a chosen people, a royal priesthood, a holy nation, God's special possession, that you may declare the praises of him who called you out of darkness into his wonderful light.*" (1 Peter 2:9)

This vocational identity means:

- Young people are created with specific gifts and callings within God's kingdom
- Their lives have meaning beyond self-fulfillment or material success
- They play a unique role in God's cosmic plan of redemption
- Their daily choices have eternal significance
- They represent Christ as His ambassadors in a broken world (2 Corinthians 5:20)

This purpose-driven identity counters the meaninglessness and nihilism prevalent in contemporary youth culture.

6. Part of God's Family, Not Isolated Individuals

Biblical identity is always connected to community:

> "*Just as a body, though one, has many parts, but all its many parts form one body, so it is with Christ.*" (1 Corinthians 12:12)

> "*Consequently, you are no longer foreigners and strangers, but fellow citizens with God's people and also members of his household.*" (Ephesians 2:19)

This communal identity means:

- Young people belong to something larger than themselves
- Their individualistic isolation can be healed through genuine Christian community
- They have a place where they truly belong, regardless of social status
- They are essential, contributing members of Christ's body with specific functions
- They find their identity in relation to others, not in isolation

This corporate identity addresses the epidemic of loneliness plaguing many young people today.

7. Eternal Beings on a Temporal Journey

Biblical identity extends beyond this present life:

> "*For here we do not have an enduring city, but we are looking for the city that is to come.*" (Hebrews 13:14)

> *"Set your minds on things above, not on earthly things. For you died, and your life is now hidden with Christ in God."* (Colossians 3:2-3)

This eternal perspective means:

- Young people are more than their current circumstances and struggles
- Their true citizenship is in heaven (Philippians 3:20)
- Their current challenges exist within the context of eternal hope
- Their identity transcends the changing seasons of biological development
- Their lives are part of God's eternal story, not merely a brief physical existence

This eternal identity provides perspective on temporary trials and temptations.

Practical Application for Parents

Nurturing biblical identity requires:

1. **Consistent Truth-Telling:** Regularly affirming these identity truths from Scripture
   > *"These commandments that I give you today are to be on your hearts. Impress them on your children. Talk about them when you sit at home and when you walk along the road, when you lie down and when you get up."* (Deuteronomy 6:6-7)

2. **Counter-Narrative Awareness:** Helping young people recognize competing identity narratives
   > *"See to it that no one takes you captive through hollow and deceptive philosophy, which depends on human tradition and the elemental spiritual forces of this world rather than on Christ."* (Colossians 2:8)

3. **Community Reinforcement:** Ensuring these truths are echoed in church and Christian community

    "*And let us consider how we may spur one another on toward love and good deeds, not giving up meeting together, as some are in the habit of doing, but encouraging one another, and all the more as you see the Day approaching.*" (Hebrews 10:24-25)

4. **Grace-Based Relationship:** Modeling unconditional love that reflects God's acceptance

    "*Accept one another, then, just as Christ accepted you, in order to bring praise to God.*" (Romans 15:7)

5. **Identity-Forming Practices:** Establishing habits that reinforce who they are in Christ

    "*Do not conform to the pattern of this world, but be transformed by the renewing of your mind. Then you will be able to test and approve what God's will is, his good, pleasing and perfect will.*" (Romans 12:2)

6. **Celebration of Uniqueness:** Affirming God's specific design of their temperament and gifts

    "*For just as each of us has one body with many members, and these members do not all have the same function, so in Christ we, though many, form one body, and each member belongs to all the others. We have different gifts, according to the grace given to each of us.*" (Romans 12:4-6a)

7. **Patient Process-Orientation:** Understanding identity formation as a journey, not an instant transformation

    "*And we all, who with unveiled faces contemplate the Lord's glory, are being transformed into his image with ever-increasing glory, which comes from the Lord, who is the Spirit.*" (2 Corinthians 3:18)

When young people internalize these biblical identity truths, they develop resilience against cultural pressures and a foundation for healthy spiritual formation that can carry them through adolescence and beyond.

Words of Encouragement:

The world your child is growing up in looks genuinely different from the one you were shaped by, and it is right to take that seriously. The digital landscape, the pace of cultural change, the mental health pressures, the worldview confusion, these are not parental anxieties looking for a target. They are real, and the parent who names them clearly is better equipped to engage them than the parent who minimizes them or is paralyzed by them.

But here is what does not change. The God who formed your child before they were born knew every detail of the world they would enter. Scripture declares: "I make known the end from the beginning, from ancient times, what is still to come" (Isaiah 46:10). God was not caught off guard by the smartphone. He was not surprised by social media or the mental health crisis or the collapse of shared cultural values. He knew the world your child would inhabit, and He placed them in it with intention and purpose.

That does not mean the challenges are not real. It means they are not outside God's reach. The Jesus who walked through a culture of Roman occupation, religious confusion, and political instability and who spoke truth that cut through all of it is the same Jesus your child needs today. "Jesus Christ is the same yesterday and today and forever" (Hebrews 13:8). The pressures are new. The anchor is not.

Your awareness of what your child is facing is already significant. Many parents look but do not see, hear but do not understand. The fact that you are reading this resource, that you are taking seriously the world your child actually inhabits rather than the one you wish they inhabited, is itself an act of love. "She watches over the affairs of her household and does not eat the bread of idleness" (Proverbs 31:27). That attentiveness matters. It is the beginning of everything else.

When you feel overwhelmed by how much ground there is to cover, remember the promise that was given not to perfect parents but to faithful ones: "For I know the plans I have for you, declares the Lord, plans to prosper you and not to harm you, plans to give you hope and a future" (Jeremiah 29:11). That promise belongs to your child. Your job is not to protect them from every challenge their generation faces. It is to make sure they know the One who holds their future in every season, including this one.

3. 3rd Culture Kids: Their Unique Struggle is Real

"I have learned, in whatever state I am, to be content. I know how to be brought low, and I know how to abound." (Philippians 4:11-12)

Every child navigates the process of forming an identity, learning who they are, where they belong, and what they believe. But for a growing population of children and young adults, that process unfolds across countries, cultures, languages, and continents. They move before they are old enough to choose. They say goodbye before they know how to grieve. They carry worlds inside them that the people around them cannot see or even understand.

These young people are often called Third Culture Kids, a term that has become widely recognized in research and cross-cultural literature over the past several decades.[1] For the purposes of this resource, we use the term 3rd Culture Kids (3CKs) to describe children and young adults who spend a significant portion of their developmental years, between ages 0 and 18, living outside their parents' passport country as a result of their family's vocation or calling.

This chapter exists because their struggle is real, it is often invisible, and it is frequently misunderstood, even by the parents who love them most.

[1] *The foundational academic research on Third Culture Kids was developed by sociologist Ruth Hill Useem and later expanded by David C. Pollock and Ruth Van Reken. Steadfast Resources acknowledges this body of work as the foundation of the broader field while presenting original frameworks for faith-integrated family application.*

Who Are 3rd Culture Kids?

A 3rd Culture Kid inhabits a space between worlds. Their parents carry one cultural identity, the passport country, the home culture, the "first culture." The country in which the family lives carries another, the host culture, the "second culture." The child, having grown up absorbing pieces of both without fully belonging to either, develops a third space all their own: a rich but often rootless blend of experiences, loyalties, and perspectives that don't fit neatly into any single national or cultural box.

This is not a deficiency. In many ways it is a profound gift. 3CKs often develop extraordinary cross-cultural empathy, linguistic agility, global awareness, and an instinctive ability to connect with people very different from themselves. But the same mobility that builds those strengths also carries a heavy cost, and that cost is most acutely felt during the developmental years when identity, belonging, and attachment are being formed.

The Four Families: Who This Chapter Serves

3CKs emerge from many different kinds of internationally mobile families. While their specific contexts differ, four primary family types make up the majority of the 3CK population this chapter addresses:

- **Missionary and Ministry Families**: Parents serving in cross-cultural ministry, church planting, humanitarian aid, or faith-based NGO work. These families often move frequently and to locations with significant cultural distance from their home country. Children may grow up in communities that are deeply sacrificial and faith-saturated, yet also isolated, under-resourced, or carrying the weight of ministry expectations.

- **Military Families**: Parents serving in armed forces, often relocated every two to three years to domestic and international postings. Military 3CKs carry a unique combination of structured community (base life) and repeated loss (the PCS cycle). They often develop remarkable resilience alongside a deep, unnamed grief from goodbyes that compound over years.

- **Corporate and Expatriate Families**: Parents working internationally for multinational corporations, NGOs, or international development organizations. These families frequently have access to international schools and expat communities, which can create a somewhat protected "bubble" that paradoxically intensifies the 3CK experience by limiting genuine host-culture integration.

- **Diplomatic Families**: Parents serving in foreign service, embassy postings, or government international roles. Diplomatic 3CKs often experience high visibility and social expectation alongside frequent rotation. The combination of privilege and rootlessness is a distinctive feature of this group.

While these four populations differ in important ways, and those distinctions are addressed later in this chapter, they share enough common 3CK experience that the core guidance here applies across all four contexts.

Understanding the 3CK Experience: What Your Child Is Carrying

To parent a 3CK well, it helps to understand the specific emotional and developmental terrain they navigate. What follows is not a clinical diagnosis but a pastoral description a window into the interior world of children who are rarely asked to articulate what they carry.

Cumulative, Unresolved Grief

Every international move involves loss. A home. A school. A neighborhood. Close friendships. A church community. A language. A sense of normalcy. For most children in internationally mobile families, these losses accumulate across multiple moves before they are emotionally or developmentally equipped to process them.

Because the family is often moving toward something exciting; a new country, a new assignment, a new adventure, grief is frequently minimized, rushed, or bypassed entirely. Children pick up the emotional cue that sadness is not welcome in the narrative of the move. Over time, unprocessed grief can harden into a protective detachment: a subconscious decision to stop investing deeply in people and places because the cost of losing them is too high.

> "*He heals the brokenhearted and binds up their wounds.*" (Psalm 147:3)

Identity Without an Anchor

"Where are you from?" is one of the most disorienting questions a 3CK can be asked. It seems simple. For them, it is anything but. The honest answer involves multiple countries, multiple homes, and a complex internal negotiation about which parts of which cultures they actually belong to.

During the years when identity is most actively forming, roughly ages 10 through 24, the precise window this resource addresses, the absence of a stable cultural anchor can generate deep anxiety about who they are, who they are allowed to be, and whether any community will ever truly be theirs. This is not a spiritual crisis; it is an identity crisis with spiritual dimensions. The two require different responses from parents.

The Hidden Nature of the Struggle

One of the most important things parents of 3CKs need to understand is that their child's struggle is often invisible to the people around them, including, sometimes, to the child themselves.

3CKs are typically articulate, globally aware, and socially skilled. They learn early how to read rooms, adapt to new environments, and present a capable face to the world. This adaptability is a genuine strength. It is also a mask. Parents who are watching for obvious distress signals may miss the quiet, gradual erosion of rootedness happening beneath a confident exterior.

The warning signs for 3CK distress look different from other at-risk indicators. They are addressed specifically in the next section of this chapter.

A Biblical Perspective on Cross-Cultural Life

Scripture is not silent on the experience of living between worlds. The people of God have always been, in some sense, people without a permanent home. Abraham left everything familiar at God's call and "went out, not knowing where he was going" (Hebrews 11:8). The Israelites spent forty years in a wilderness between a home they had left and a home they had not yet reached. The early church scattered across cultures and continents, carrying the gospel into foreign soil.

This does not make the 3CK experience painless. But it does mean that the God your child is invited to trust is not a stranger to displacement, cultural liminality, or the grief of leaving. He entered a world that was not His home and made it His dwelling anyway. That is not a distant theological fact, it is the lived reality of the incarnate Christ, and it is a genuine comfort to offer your 3CK child at the right moment.

> "*For here we have no lasting city, but we seek the city that is to come.*" (Hebrews 13:14)

The Abandonment Wound

There is a particular form of grief that deserves specific attention across all internationally mobile families. In some situations, a parent's assignment takes them to a location that is deemed too dangerous, too remote, or too demanding to bring the family along. A corporate assignee may be sent to a two-year posting while their spouse and children remain in the home country. A missionary family may separate for the sake of the children's education or safety. A military parent may deploy for extended periods while the family stays behind. In each of these situations, the child is left to grow up with a parent who is physically absent for months or years at a time.

The child may understand intellectually why the separation happened. They may have been told that the work is important, that the sacrifice is meaningful, that the family will be reunited. What the child often cannot fully process is the emotional reality beneath that understanding: they have been left. The people whose presence is the foundation of their safety are not there. And no amount of explanation fully resolves the ache of a child growing up without both parents in the room.

This is not a failure of parenting. It is a wound, and it needs to be named. Children who carry it often develop a protective self-sufficiency that looks like resilience from the outside while masking a deep reluctance to trust or depend on anyone. For children in faith-based families, the spiritual dimension of this wound can be particularly complex. If a child has learned early that the people who love them most will leave when the calling or the career demands it, that experience can unconsciously shape how they understand a God who asks for full surrender.

Parents who have made this kind of separation decision, or who are considering it, should approach it with clear eyes about the cost their child may bear, and with a commitment to create sustained, intentional reconnection when the family is together. Children who have experienced this separation need explicit permission to grieve it honestly, without being asked to frame it as sacrifice, calling, or simply the way things are. The grief belongs to them.

Bullying in Host Countries: The Invisible Wound

There is a dimension of the 3CK experience that rarely surfaces in family conversations, that children almost never volunteer, and that parents, absorbed in the enormous logistics of international life, can miss entirely. Many 3CK children are bullied in their host countries. Not occasionally, and not mildly. For some, it is a defining and deeply wounding feature of their international childhood, one that shapes their sense of safety, identity, and belonging for years after the family has moved on.

This is not widely discussed in expatriate or missionary communities, in part because the international life narrative tends toward adventure, growth, and opportunity. The image of a child being targeted, excluded, or harassed in a foreign school because of how they look, how they speak, or where they come from does not fit comfortably into that narrative. As a result, children learn very early that this part of their experience is not welcome in the family story, and so they carry it silently, alone, while performing the role of the adaptable, resilient, globally-minded child that their family and community expect.

Parents need to know this. Not to be alarmed, but to be alert, and to create the kind of deliberate, non-anxious space in which a child who has been suffering quietly finally feels safe enough to say so.

Why 3CK Children Are Targeted

Bullying tends to target difference, and 3CK children arrive in host countries carrying visible difference on every level. Their accent, their appearance, their cultural references, their clothing, their food, all of it can mark them as outsiders in environments where outsiders are not always welcomed. The specific form the targeting takes varies by context, but several patterns are common across 3CK populations:

- **Language-based exclusion and mockery**: Children who speak the host country's language imperfectly, or not at all during the initial transition, are frequent targets. Peers may mimic their accent, deliberately speak too quickly to exclude them, or refuse to interact with them altogether. This is particularly acute in non-international school environments where the child is the only foreign student in the class.

- **Racial and ethnic targeting**: Children whose physical appearance differs from the dominant population in their host country are vulnerable to race-based targeting. This can be particularly disorienting for children who did not experience racial otherness in their passport country and have no relational framework for processing it. The wound is doubled when parents, unfamiliar with this dimension of the host culture, do not immediately recognize what their child is describing.

- **Anti-Western or anti-American sentiment**: In many parts of the world, Western and particularly American families carry the political and cultural weight of their home country's global reputation, regardless of their own personal views or character. Children can find themselves targeted not for anything they have done but for what they represent in the eyes of peers and community. This form of bullying can be especially confusing for children who love their host country and feel genuinely at home there.

- **Faith-based targeting**: Children in missionary and ministry families are at particular risk of faith-based targeting in host countries with majority non-Christian religious cultures. Being known as the child of a Christian worker or being identifiably Christian in a context where that is a minority or stigmatized identity, can make a child a target for social exclusion, ridicule, or in some contexts, direct hostility. Parents should approach this with both pastoral honesty and genuine courage, grounding their child in the scriptural reality that following Jesus has always carried social cost (John 15:18-19) while also taking the practical safety dimensions seriously.

- **Privilege-based resentment**: Corporate and diplomatic families in particular may find that their standard of living creates visible economic disparity between their children and local peers. Children may be excluded, mocked, or resented for their perceived wealth, access, or privilege, a form of social targeting that is especially painful because the child often does not experience themselves as privileged and may genuinely love and identify with the host culture.

Why Children Don't Tell Their Parents

Understanding why 3CK children typically remain silent about host-country bullying is as important as understanding the bullying itself. Several dynamics conspire to keep the wound hidden:

- **Not wanting to burden parents who have already sacrificed**: Children in ministry and military families especially tend to be acutely aware of what their parents have given up. Adding to that weight by reporting their own suffering can feel selfish or disloyal to a child who loves their family deeply.

- **Fear that disclosure will force another move**: Children who have already experienced multiple moves may fear that revealing a serious problem at school will trigger yet another uprooting, losing what little community they have managed to establish alongside the place where the bullying is happening. The calculation, however painful, can feel like a reason for silence.

- **Shame and self-blame**: Children who are targeted for being foreign may internalize the message that being foreign is the problem, that if they could only adapt faster, speak better, look more local, belong more convincingly, the targeting would stop. This self-blame is both common and deeply damaging, and it often intensifies with age.

- **Limited avenues for reporting**: In local (non-international) schools, the child may not have the language proficiency to report bullying to teachers or school administration effectively. Cultural norms around conflict, authority, and peer relationships vary significantly, and in some host cultures, involving adults in peer conflicts carries its own social consequences that make reporting feel more dangerous than the bullying itself.

Warning Signs That Your Child May Be Experiencing Bullying

- **Reluctance or refusal to attend school**: Complaints of physical illness (stomachaches, headaches) that resolve on weekends or school holidays are a classic indicator that something painful is happening in the school environment specifically.

- **Sudden rejection of the host culture**: A child who previously showed interest in the host country's language, food, or culture and who abruptly refuses engagement with all of it may be processing rejection from within that culture rather than genuine disinterest.

- **Withdrawal and increased isolation**: Spending increasing amounts of time alone at home, declining invitations or activities, and showing no interest in building local friendships may indicate that peer relationships in the host country have become a source of pain rather than connection.

- **Unexplained changes in mood around school transitions**: Anxiety, irritability, or low mood that appears on Sunday evenings and intensifies on school mornings, then eases on Friday afternoons, warrants a direct, gentle inquiry into what school is actually like on a daily basis.

- **Negative self-talk about identity**: Comments like "I hate being American," "I wish I looked like them," or "I don't fit in anywhere" can be the surface expression of bullying-related shame that the child has not been able to name directly.

- **Heightened interest in leaving the host country**: While some desire to move on is normal in internationally mobile children, a sudden and intense preoccupation with when the family will leave, particularly in a child who previously seemed settled, can indicate that something has changed in their social environment that makes remaining feel unsafe.

✈ FROM THE FIELD

Our oldest daughter was being bullied in Colombia, mocked in Spanish she was still learning, her things stolen, the girls in her class systematically unkind. My wife witnessed it directly at one point and intervened. The bullying continued anyway. Our daughter never told us.

What we learned from her teachers was that she had quietly appointed herself the protector of the smaller children in her class who couldn't stand up for themselves. She was handling it the way we had raised her to handle it.

We had a rule in our home about conflict. You first try to talk to the person directly. If that doesn't work, you bring it to your

> *teacher. If that doesn't work, go to the administrator. And if the people in authority still fail to act, you have every right to defend yourself and take action. Their failure to protect you is not your responsibility. They are in authority for a reason, and if they are not using it to protect you, you have to protect yourself.*
>
> *She had followed the rule. She had tried every step. And when the system failed her, she stood her ground -- not only for herself, but for the children around her who had no one else.*
>
> *That is what a child looks like when she has internalized her family's values so completely that she applies them alone, without fanfare, in the middle of a world that is not cooperating.*

How Parents Can Respond

- **Ask directly and without alarm**: Many children will not volunteer information about bullying, but they will answer a calm, specific, direct question. Rather than "Is everything okay at school?", which invites a yes/no and almost always gets "fine", try: "Sometimes when kids come from a different country, other kids can be unkind about it. Has anything like that happened to you?" The specificity signals safety. It communicates that you already understand this is possible, that you are not going to be shocked, and that there is room in your relationship for an honest answer.

- **Believe them fully and immediately**: When a child finally discloses that they are being bullied, the most critical parental response in the first moments is complete belief and full presence. Resist the impulse to minimize ("Kids can be like that"), problem-solve prematurely ("Have you tried just ignoring them?"), or question details. Sit with them in the reality of what they have just trusted you with. The child who felt they could not tell you for months has just taken an enormous risk. Honor it.

- **Counter the shame with truth**: Explicitly dismantle the self-blame narrative. Tell your child clearly: being different is not the problem. Being targeted for difference is a failure of the people doing the targeting, not of the child being targeted. Then ground that truth biblically: God knit your child together in their mother's womb (Psalm 139:13-14), their appearance, their background, their passport, their accent, all of it was known and chosen before they took their first breath. No peer's cruelty can undo what God has declared: they are fearfully and wonderfully made.

- **Engage the school with cultural intelligence**: Approach the school through the cultural norms of the host country rather than importing the conflict resolution expectations of your passport country. How a school in one country expects parents to engage with concerns about peer behavior may be very different from what works in another. Where possible, enlist a trusted local adult, a community contact, a national colleague, a church member, who can advise on how to approach the school effectively. If the school environment is unsafe and cannot be adequately addressed, evaluate whether a different school placement is appropriate.

- **Build a community outside the hostile environment**: If the school is the primary site of bullying, prioritize building meaningful community for your child in other contexts, an international church community, a sports team, an arts program, an expat family network. A child who has at least one environment in which they are known, welcomed, and valued can better weather hostility in another.

- **Address it before the next move**: The temptation when a posting ends is to let the move function as the resolution, a fresh start, a new place, a chance to leave the hard thing behind. Resist this. Unaddressed bullying trauma does not stay in the country where it happened; it travels with the child. Ensure that your child has had adequate opportunity to process what they experienced, with you, and where necessary with a counselor, before the next chapter begins. See Chapter 7 (Biblical Intervention Strategies) and Chapter 10 (Self-Harm) for guidance on when professional support is appropriate.

"*If the world hates you, know that it has hated me before it hated you.*" (John 15:18)

Jesus was rejected in his own hometown (Luke 4:28-29), questioned by his own people, and ultimately crucified by the culture he came to redeem. He is not a distant theological concept when your child is being targeted for being foreign, He is a Savior who was himself rejected, who bore that rejection without becoming defined by it, and who offers your child the only identity that no peer, no culture, and no hostile school environment can ever take away.

Warning Signs Specific to 3CK Youth

The warning signs outlined in Chapter 4 apply to all young people, including 3CKs. Parents of internationally mobile children should be familiar with those indicators. However, 3CKs also present a distinct set of signals that can be easy to miss or misattribute. What follows are warning signs that parents of 3CKs should watch for specifically, patterns that are common in this population and warrant prayerful, attentive response.

Emotional and Relational Warning Signs

- **Protective detachment**: Deliberate resistance to forming close friendships, sometimes disguised as social confidence or self-sufficiency. The child connects easily at a surface level but consistently avoids depth.

- **Chameleon behavior**: Rapidly and completely adopting the identity, speech, and values of whatever peer group is currently present, not as normal social adaptation but as a loss of any stable sense of self.

- **Disproportionate grief responses**: Intense emotional reactions to seemingly small losses (a pet, a friendship, a familiar routine) that may actually be the accumulated grief of multiple unmourned moves expressing itself at last.

- **Idealization of a previous country or posting**: Persistent, consuming longing for a former home that prevents engagement with present life, often intensifying around transitions or anniversaries of moves.

- **Contempt for the home country**: Particularly upon repatriation, a strong and vocal rejection of the passport country's culture, values, or people, sometimes masking a deep fear of not belonging there either.

Spiritual Warning Signs

- **Faith fatigue**: Specific to missionary and ministry family 3CKs, exhaustion with faith language, church culture, or spiritual expectations that were part of the family's international identity but feel hollow in a new context.

- **Transactional view of God**: A subconscious belief that faithfulness to God's calling should protect the family from painful moves, and when it doesn't, a quiet but serious disillusionment with both God and parents.

- **Spiritual homelessness**: Having worshipped in multiple church traditions across cultures, the 3CK may feel that no single expression of faith is fully theirs, leading to disconnection from church community as a whole.

Behavioral Warning Signs

- **Chronic restlessness**: An inability to settle, physically, relationally, vocationally, accompanied by a compulsive desire to move, change, or escape whenever life becomes stable and familiar.

- **Academic disengagement at transition points**: A pattern of strong performance that drops sharply with each new school placement, potentially misdiagnosed as a learning issue rather than a grief and adjustment response.

- **Risk-seeking behavior in new environments**: Using novelty, risk, and intensity as substitutes for the depth of connection the child has learned not to trust.

See Chapter 4 for the comprehensive Warning Signs framework applicable to all young people ages 10-24. The signs above should be read alongside - not instead of - that broader guidance.

Age-Specific Guidance for Parents of 3CKs

The 3CK experience shifts significantly across developmental stages. A child who moves at age seven carries different wounds than one who moves at fourteen. A young adult attempting to repatriate at twenty-two faces different challenges than a twelve-year-old beginning their first international posting. Age-attuned parenting is essential.

Pre-Teens and Early Adolescents (Ages 10-13)

This age group is in the early stages of forming an identity beyond their family. For 3CKs in this range, a move can feel like the ground shifting beneath them at precisely the moment they are learning to stand on it. Belonging to a peer group is becoming critically important, and international mobility makes that belonging painfully unstable.

- **Name the grief explicitly**: Children this age often do not have language for what they are feeling when they move. Give them the words: 'What you're feeling is grief, and it is completely right. We lost something real when we left.'

- **Preserve meaningful connections**: Facilitate continued contact with friends left behind; video calls, messages, letters. Teach them that relationships can survive distance, which is itself a life-giving truth for a 3CK.

- **Create cultural continuity at home**: Maintain family traditions, foods, music, and rhythms from beloved postings. The home becomes a container for identity when the outside world keeps changing.

- **Introduce biblical identity early**: Begin the foundational conversation: your identity is not in where you live, who your friends are, or what country you're from. You are known, named, and loved by God before any of those things.

- **Watch for academic withdrawal**: A sudden drop in engagement at a new school is more likely grief than ability. Communicate this clearly to teachers and school counselors.

- **Avoid minimizing the loss**: Phrases like 'You'll make new friends' or 'This is such an adventure', while well-intentioned, communicate that the child's grief is unwelcome. Sit with the sadness before moving toward hope.

Middle Adolescents (Ages 14-17)

Adolescence is the developmental season most disrupted by international mobility. Peer relationships, romantic friendships, school belonging, and identity formation are all at their peak intensity, and a move during these years can feel catastrophic to a teenager, regardless of how compelling the family's reasons for moving are.

Parents sometimes underestimate how much a move at fourteen costs their teenager. The teenager often does not have the tools to explain it and may not try. They simply go quiet, or angry, or both.

- **Give them a voice in the decision where possible**: Even when the move is non-negotiable, consulting teenagers about timing, school selection, and transition planning communicates respect for what they are losing.

- **Don't spiritualize the pain away**: For missionary and ministry family teens especially, the pressure to be grateful for the family's calling can effectively silence legitimate grief. A teen is allowed to grieve a move even if God called the family to it.

- **Connect them with other 3CK peers**: There is profound relief in meeting another teenager who understands the 'passport question' without needing it explained. Seek out international schools, expat communities, or online communities of 3CK young people.

- **Invest in identity conversations**: Who are you beyond where you've lived? What do you believe, not just what have you been taught? What matters to you? These questions, asked consistently and without agenda, build the internal foundation 3CK teens need.

- **Take the chameleon warning sign seriously**: If your teenager seems to completely reinvent themselves with each new context, that is not adaptability, it is the absence of a stable self. It warrants gentle, consistent engagement.

- **Be present through anger**: Anger directed at parents for moves is common in this age group, and some of it is legitimate. Receive it without becoming defensive. Their grief is real even when the expression is imperfect.

Late Adolescents and Young Adults (Ages 18-24)

Young adults in internationally mobile families face a distinctive convergence of challenges. They are navigating the normal developmental tasks of this season, identity consolidation, vocational direction, significant relationships, independence from family, while simultaneously carrying the accumulated weight of a globally mobile childhood that they are only now, perhaps for the first time, having the cognitive and emotional capacity to process fully.

Many 3CKs do not begin to understand the depth of their own experience until their late teens or early twenties. This is also often the season of repatriation, a transition addressed specifically in the next section.

- **Normalize the delayed processing**: It is entirely common for 3CK young adults to surface grief, anger, or confusion about their childhood years that parents had no idea was there. Receive it without defensiveness. 'Tell me more' is almost always the right response.

- **Resist the urge to defend the moves**: Parents who feel criticized may be tempted to justify the family's international life. The young adult is not necessarily questioning your decisions, they are finally grieving what those decisions cost them. These are different conversations.

- **Support vocational discernment**: 3CK young adults often struggle with vocational direction not because of lack of ability but because of lack of rootedness. Career counseling, mentorship, and spiritual direction can all be valuable.

- **Watch for chronic restlessness**: The compulsion to keep moving; changing cities, changing jobs, changing relationships, can be a way of managing the fear of putting down roots that might be pulled up again. Gentle, consistent naming of this pattern is a gift.

- **Invest in their local church connection**: Young adult 3CKs who drift from faith community often do so not from theological disbelief but from the exhaustion of building yet another community from scratch. The investment of helping them find and commit to a local church is significant.

- **Treat them as fellow adults**: Communicate respect for the maturity they have genuinely earned through global experience. Approach difficult conversations collaboratively rather than directively.

Population-Specific Considerations

While the core 3CK experience is shared across family types, each of the four populations carries distinctive features that shape how the challenge presents and how parents can respond most effectively.

Missionary and Ministry Families

Children in missionary and ministry families carry an additional layer of complexity: they did not merely move for a parent's career. They moved for God. That theological framing, however genuine and important, creates specific vulnerabilities.

- **The 'sacrifice' narrative**: Children raised in a culture that valorizes sacrifice can internalize the message that their own grief is spiritually inappropriate. Parents must actively separate the value of the calling from the legitimacy of the cost it extracted from their children.

- **Faith by association**: Ministry kids often grow up in deeply faith-saturated environments. When they leave, they must determine whether their faith is genuinely their own or a product of environment. This is healthy and necessary, and can look alarming to parents. Create space for it rather than suppressing it.
- **Spiritual exhaustion**: Teenagers who grew up serving, performing, and representing the mission may arrive at adulthood genuinely depleted. Rest, ordinary life, and faith that requires nothing of them for a season can be deeply restorative.
- **Honor their contribution**: Ministry kids gave something real for the family's calling. Name it. Thank them. Don't assume they know you see it.

Military Families

Military 3CKs have the most structured mobility experience of any group, PCS cycles are predictable in their unpredictability, base communities provide consistent social scaffolding, and the military family identity is itself a form of belonging. But the regularity of loss does not diminish its weight.

- **Acknowledge the PCS grief cycle**: Military families become skilled at efficient transitions, which can lead to bypassing emotional processing altogether. Build in intentional grief time before and after each move.

- **Guard against emotional armor**: Children who learn to not get too attached in order to protect themselves from repeated goodbyes may carry that armor into adult relationships long after the military years are over.

- **Base community as both gift and limitation**: The close community of military life is a real protective factor for 3CKs. It can also insulate children from genuine integration into local communities, creating a gap that becomes disorienting when military life ends.

- **Transition out of military life**: When a parent leaves military service and the family repatriates or settles permanently, the loss of the military community structure can be as disorienting as any international move. Plan for it intentionally.

Corporate and Expatriate Families

Corporate expat families frequently inhabit a privileged but isolating world, international schools, expat clubs, and company-provided housing can create a comfortable bubble that looks like integration but functions as separation from the actual host culture.

- **Intentional host-culture engagement**: Families that make deliberate efforts to learn the language, build relationships outside the expat community, and engage genuinely with local culture provide their children with a richer, more grounded international experience.

- **The 'golden cage' dynamic**: High salaries, luxury accommodations, and corporate benefits can make it difficult to acknowledge the real costs of expat life. The material comfort does not negate the emotional challenge, and children in these families may feel guilty for struggling.

- **School transitions**: International schools serve 3CKs well in many respects, but they also create a community almost entirely composed of people who are leaving. The chronic goodbye culture of international schools is its own unique grief ecosystem.

- **When the contract ends**: Corporate postings typically end on a predetermined schedule or at a company's discretion. Families should begin transition preparation well in advance of departure, both logistically and emotionally.

Diplomatic Families

Diplomatic children live at the intersection of privilege and pressure. Their parent's public role often carries social expectations that extend to the entire family, how they present, what they say, who they associate with.

- **The performance dimension**: Diplomatic children learn early that their behavior reflects on their parent's professional standing. This can generate significant anxiety and a persistent sense that authenticity is dangerous.

- **Security and privacy constraints**: Some diplomatic postings involve genuine security concerns that limit children's freedom, social contact, and normal adolescent independence. These constraints are real and their psychological weight should be acknowledged.

- **High-visibility transitions**: When a posting ends, the transition is often public and abrupt. Children do not always have the opportunity to say proper goodbyes or process the ending before the next chapter begins.

- **Identity beyond the title**: Children of diplomats sometimes struggle to develop an identity independent of their parent's prominent role. Intentional cultivation of their own interests, gifts, and relationships is important.

Repatriation: When Home Feels Foreign

Of all the transitions in a 3CK's life, repatriation, returning to the family's passport country after years abroad, is frequently the most disorienting. And it is the one that parents are least prepared for, because it looks like it should be easy. You are going home. The language is familiar. The culture is supposedly yours.

For a 3CK who has grown up abroad, none of those things are actually true in the way the adults around them assume. The passport country is not home in any meaningful felt sense. The language may be fluent, but the cultural references, the social norms, the unspoken rules of peer interaction, these are all foreign. And unlike an international move to a new country, where everyone acknowledges the adaptation required, repatriation comes with an invisible expectation that no adjustment should be necessary at all.

This expectation is one of the most isolating features of the repatriation experience. 3CKs who struggle to readjust to their passport country often feel they are not permitted to say so, because they are "home."

Why Repatriation Is Hard

- **Reverse culture shock**: Culture shock upon entering a foreign country is expected and acknowledged. Reverse culture shock, the disorientation of returning to a culture you are supposed to belong to, is real but socially invisible. It can be more destabilizing than the original move abroad precisely because there is no permission structure to struggle.

- **Peer disconnection**: Peers in the passport country have shared experiences, cultural touchstones, social histories, and relational networks that the returning 3CK does not share. The 3CK may feel more foreign in their own country than they ever did abroad.

- **The loss of international identity**: Many 3CKs build a significant part of their identity around being "the one who has lived overseas." Repatriation removes that distinguishing feature and leaves a vacuum that must be filled with something new.

- **Grief for the country left behind**: Repatriation means leaving a place and community that was genuinely home in an experiential sense, even if not on paper. That loss is real and deserves the same acknowledgment as any other significant loss.

- **Family system stress**: Repatriation affects the whole family simultaneously, parents are also readjusting, which can reduce the emotional bandwidth available to attune to children's needs. Families who recognize this dynamic in advance are better equipped to navigate it.

Practical Guidance for the Repatriation Transition

- **Name the transition explicitly**: Don't let repatriation be treated as a non-event. Acknowledge what is being left, what is being entered, and that the adjustment will take real time.

- **Build in a transition window**: Where possible, allow for a period of lower expectations; academically, socially, professionally, during the initial repatriation phase. For children and teens, this may mean a semester of grace before assessing academic performance. For young adults, it may mean not rushing vocational decisions.

- **Connect with others who understand**: Other repatriated families, 3CK communities, or international school alumni networks can provide the validating experience of being understood. Online communities of 3CK young people can be especially valuable for teenagers and young adults who feel alone in their experience.

- **Don't rush the grieving**: The grief of repatriation is legitimate, and it takes time. Parents who grew up in one place their entire lives may underestimate how long the adjustment actually takes. Years, not weeks, is a more realistic frame.

- **Seek professional support when needed**: If a young person's repatriation adjustment is significantly disrupting their functioning; academically, relationally, spiritually, professional support from a counselor familiar with cross-cultural transition is appropriate and valuable. See Chapter 6 for guidance on when and how to seek additional help.

"*Be strong and courageous. Do not be frightened, and do not be dismayed, for the Lord your God is with you wherever you go.*" (Joshua 1:9)

Heart-Focused Parenting for the 3CK Journey

The principles in Chapter 5, reaching the heart behind the behavior, asking questions rather than issuing corrections, creating a climate of grace, are especially vital for parents of 3CKs. The concerning behaviors in 3CK young people almost always have roots that go deeper and further back than the behavior itself suggests. A teenager who appears withdrawn, angry, or rootless is almost certainly carrying grief that has never been named.

What Your 3CK Child Needs Most From You

- **Acknowledgment before advice**: Before offering solutions, perspective, or spiritual framing, simply acknowledge what your child has experienced and what it has cost them. 'I know this has been hard. I see that.' These words are not weakness; they are the open door through which everything else eventually becomes possible.

- **Stability in the midst of change**: You cannot always control where the family moves. You can control the quality of presence, warmth, and consistency you bring to your child regardless of the zip code. You are the constant when everything else changes.

- **Permission to grieve**: Explicitly give your child permission to be sad, angry, and confused about the international life you have led. Their grief does not invalidate your calling. It simply means they are human and they have loved the people and places you have lived among.

- **A theology of belonging**: The deepest answer to the 3CK identity question is not a country, a community, or a culture - it is a Person. Consistently pointing your child to an identity grounded in Christ, known before the foundation of the world, held by a Father who does not move, belonging to a kingdom that transcends every border, is the most durable gift you can give them.

- **Your own emotional honesty**: 3CK children are exceptionally perceptive. They read the gap between what their parents say ("This is an adventure!") and what they feel (grief, stress, ambivalence). Parents who model honest emotional processing, including their own sadness about what the family has left behind, give their children permission to do the same.

Action Steps for Parents

1. **Have the conversation you have been avoiding.**

   If you have not explicitly acknowledged the cost of your family's international life to your child, do it. It is not too late. A simple, sincere conversation, "I know our moves have been hard. I want you to know I see that, and I'm sorry for the parts of it that hurt you", can open doors that have been closed for years.

2. **Learn your child's specific story.**

   What posting did they love most? What goodbye cost them most? What do they miss? What are they afraid of? Ask the questions and listen without redirecting. Their story is worth knowing in detail.

3. **Build rituals of remembrance.**

   Create family practices that honor the places you have lived and the people you have loved across the world. A map with pins. A meal from a former posting. An annual letter to a friend left behind. These are small things that communicate to your child: what you loved was worth loving, and we do not forget.

4. **Connect them with a stable faith community.**

   Wherever you are, prioritize finding a church community that your 3CK child can invest in and be known by. The local church, imperfect as it always is, is one of the most powerful stabilizing forces available to a young person whose world keeps moving.

5. **Seek specialized support when needed.**

   Counselors, mentors, and support communities that specialize in cross-cultural transition and 3CK experience exist and are worth seeking out. Steadfast Resources will soon maintain a network of 3CK-informed counselors and family coaches available at https://steadfastresources.com/3ck-support. The Seekers International Foundation can connect families with local support through https://iseekers.org.

Scripture Based Prayers for 3CK Families

- **For rootedness in Christ**: "Lord, may my child be rooted and grounded in love, and may they have strength to comprehend the breadth and length and height and depth of your love that surpasses knowledge." (Ephesians 3:17-19)

- **For the grief of leaving**: "Father, you are close to the brokenhearted and you save those who are crushed in spirit. Be near to my child in every goodbye." (Psalm 34:18)

- **For identity in a new place**: "You know my child by name. You formed them before any country or culture shaped them. Let them find their deepest belonging in You." (Isaiah 43:1)

- **For the repatriation journey**: "Lord, give my child courage to enter what feels foreign, and make what feels foreign feel like home in time. You go before them." (Joshua 1:9)

- **For the parent carrying the weight**: "When I am overwhelmed, lead me to the rock that is higher than I. I cannot carry this alone, and I was never meant to." (Psalm 61:2)

Words of Encouragement:

You have said yes to something costly. Whether God called you to the mission field, your country called you to serve, your company sent you abroad, or you simply followed the path that opened before you, you have raised your children in the in-between places, the threshold spaces, the countries that were never quite home. That was not a small thing. It asked something real of your children, and it has asked something real of you. God sees all of it. The psalmist wrote that God keeps count of every restless night, that He collects every tear in a bottle and records each one in His book (Psalm 56:8). Not one goodbye your child has grieved, not one friendship abandoned by a move, not one night they cried in a new bedroom in a new country has been lost or forgotten before Him. He is the God who notices, who remembers, and who holds what we cannot hold ourselves.

Scripture is full of people who were carried somewhere they did not choose and shaped into something they could not have become any other way. Joseph was taken from his family and his homeland while still a teenager. He lost his name, his freedom, and every anchor of belonging he had ever known, and yet at the end of his story, he could say with tears streaming down his face, "It was not you who sent me here, but God" (Genesis 45:8). He did not say the pain wasn't real. He said God was in it anyway. The hall of faith in Hebrews 11 is lined with men and women who "went out, not knowing where they were going" (v. 8), who "acknowledged that they were strangers and exiles on the earth" (v. 13), and who died still holding promises they had not yet received, because they had learned that the God who called them was more reliable than the ground beneath their feet. This is the inheritance your internationally mobile life is pressing into your children, whether they can name it yet or not. You are raising people who know, at a bone-deep level, that belonging cannot be found in an address.

That is not a wound to be fixed. In God's hands, it is the beginning of wisdom.

When God spoke to the exiles in Babylon, a people displaced, grieving, far from everything that had given their lives meaning, He did not tell them their pain was unimportant. He told them to plant gardens and build houses and pray for the city where He had sent them (Jeremiah 29:5-7). And then He said, "For I know the plans I have for you... plans to prosper you and not to harm you, plans to give you hope and a future" (v. 11). Those words were not spoken to people in comfort. They were spoken to people in exile, people who understood displacement in a way that most never will. If your child is struggling today, if the repatriation is harder than anyone warned you it would be, if the accumulated goodbyes have finally surfaced and the grief is bigger than you expected, take those words for yourself and for your child. God is not absent from the exile. He authored a future for His people from within it. He will do the same for yours. "The one who calls you is faithful, and he will do it" (1 Thessalonians 5:24). Keep moving forward. The harvest from the seeds you are planting in your child's life, will come; in God's time, in ways you cannot yet see, through a journey that was never wasted.

4. Warning Signs: Identifying At-Risk Behaviors

The following warning signs may manifest differently depending on your child's age and development. We've organized them by category, with notes on age-specific considerations where relevant.

The warning signs in this chapter are real and knowing them matters. But the most powerful thing a parent can do is not wait for warning signs to appear. The families who navigate cross-cultural transitions with the greatest resilience are not the ones who responded best to crisis. They are the ones who built something before the crisis arrived.

Preemptive parenting is not about eliminating difficulty. It is about building the relational infrastructure that gives your child somewhere to bring their pain before it finds another way out. That infrastructure is built in the ordinary moments: the consistent one-on-one time, the dinner table conversations that go beyond schedules and grades, the bedtime check-ins that stay open long enough for something real to surface. It is built through a family culture that normalizes struggle rather than shaming it, that treats doubt and difficulty as things to be brought to the table rather than hidden from it.

Early communication is the foundation of that culture. A child who has been consistently invited to share hard things when they are small will be more likely to share hard things when they are large. The question is not whether your child will face difficulty. They will. The question is whether the pathway between their inner world and yours has been kept open. That pathway is built long before a crisis demands it.

The warning signs that follow are organized to help you recognize when something significant may be developing beneath the surface. But read them as a parent who is already investing in the foundation, not as a parent who is searching for problems. The goal is not vigilance. The goal is connection.

✈ FROM THE FIELD

My youngest daughter had an extraordinarily high pain threshold, and she had learned early that telling us she was hurt sometimes meant being kept inside. So, she stopped telling us. She fell, she bumped into things, she got hurt, and she brushed it off and kept going. We accepted this as part of her personality.

What we did not know was that in Colombia, a child at her school had stabbed her. A teacher found her, cleaned and bandaged the wound, obtained a new school uniform, and disposed of the old one. My daughter never said a word to us. We never knew it happened.

After we repatriated, she fell at a playground and said nothing. Several weeks passed before she mentioned, almost in passing, that her leg was hurting. We knew immediately that if she was saying something, it had to be serious. When we looked, the infection had traveled from her knee to her thigh. The hospital sent us home with medication. Her pediatrician, furious, called them back and told them that if anything happened to this little girl, they would be held responsible. It was MRSA. She spent a month in the hospital.

A child who has learned to hide pain will hide it until they find another way to release it. The warning sign was not the infection; it was the pattern of silence that had been building for years. We had accepted that pattern as a personality trait. It almost cost us her life.

Understanding What Drives At-Risk Behavior

Before examining specific warning signs, it is important to understand what is often driving them. In most cases, the concerning behaviors you observe in your child are not the core problem. They are a response to something deeper. Research consistently shows that a significant portion of at-risk behavior in adolescents is rooted in trauma. Trauma does not always arrive as a single dramatic event. It can accumulate quietly through repeated experiences of loss, rejection, displacement, or unresolved pain. For internationally mobile children, the cumulative weight of multiple transitions, cultural disorientation, and the grief of leaving people and places behind can create a trauma burden that remains invisible to everyone around them, including the child carrying it.

When a child has been carrying unspoken pain for an extended period, the warning signs you observe are often not the beginning of something new. They are the moment the pain found another outlet. Self-harm, substance use, emotional withdrawal, and sudden behavioral shifts are frequently attempts to manage overwhelming internal distress that has no other place to go. The child is not broken and they are not beyond reach. They are communicating in the only language available to them in that moment. The question a parent must learn to ask is not "what is wrong with my child?" but "what has happened to my child?"

Not every concerning behavior, however, is a trauma response. Some behavior is genuine rebellion, and the two require different responses. Treating trauma as rebellion, responding with discipline, confrontation, or spiritual pressure alone, can deepen the wound and drive the pain further underground. But treating rebellion as trauma, offering acceptance without accountability, does the child a different kind of harm. Learning to distinguish between the two is one of the most important skills a parent can develop. As a general guide: when behavior is sudden, escalating, and accompanied by emotional withdrawal, trauma is more likely the driver. When behavior is persistent, selective, and accompanied by open defiance without apparent distress, genuine rebellion deserves more direct attention. The chapters that follow will help you develop that discernment.

When trauma is present and your child is not communicating the underlying pain, you cannot always get to the root of it alone. Children who have learned to hide their pain are often remarkably skilled at presenting a functioning exterior while carrying significant internal distress. If you observe the warning signs in this chapter and your child is not responding to your attempts to connect and communicate, seeking the help of a trained counselor is not a sign of parental failure. It is an act of wisdom. A skilled clinician can create the safety and structure that allows a child to begin uncovering what they cannot yet bring to you. Your role in that process is to stay close, remain non-judgmental, and be ready to receive what surfaces when it does.

As you read through the warning signs that follow, it is important to hold them with discernment rather than alarm. Many of the behaviors listed can appear within normal adolescent development. Concern increases when these behaviors become persistent, extreme, impairing, secretive, or self-destructive, or when they appear in clusters rather than in isolation. A single behavior observed once is rarely a warning sign. A pattern of behaviors that persists across time and domains is worth paying close attention to. The goal of this chapter is not to make you afraid of your child's development. It is to help you recognize when something more than development may be at work.

Changes in Spiritual Life

Before reading the spiritual warning signs that follow, it is important to hold them with particular care. Adolescence is a season when young people naturally begin differentiating from the belief systems they inherited from their parents. Theological questioning, spiritual ambivalence, temporary disengagement from religious practices, and even expressions of doubt are a normal and often necessary part of developing a faith that is genuinely one's own rather than simply borrowed. These experiences should not automatically be interpreted as rebellion, spiritual failure, or signs of crisis.

For some teenagers, particularly those ages 10 and older, this differentiation takes a more deliberate form. They may feel that their parents' faith was placed on them without their consent, that they were raised inside a belief system they never chose, and that pulling away is the only way to find out who they actually are. This is not always a rejection of God. It is often a rejection of a faith that never felt like theirs. Parents who respond to this with fear, pressure, or shame tend to push their children further away. Parents who respond with openness, honest conversation, and a willingness to let their child ask hard questions without penalty tend to find that the door stays open even when the child steps back.

Spiritual changes become a genuine concern when they occur alongside other warning indicators such as hopelessness, severe isolation, self-hatred, expressions of worthlessness, trauma symptoms, or self-destructive behavior. A teenager who stops attending youth group while also withdrawing from every relationship and expressing that life has no meaning is presenting a very different picture from one who is simply wrestling with hard theological questions. The warning signs below are intended to help parents recognize the difference. Spiritual questioning alone is not a warning sign. It is a conversation waiting to happen.

- **Sudden Disinterest in Faith**: Refusing to attend church or engage in spiritual conversations
  - *Age Consideration*: Younger children (10-13) might express this through complaints or resistance, while older teens may be more direct in their refusal
- **Cynicism About Christianity**: Expressing contempt or mockery toward beliefs they once held

  - *Age Consideration*: This often emerges more strongly in middle adolescence (14-17) as critical thinking develops

- **Significant Theological Shifts**: Adopting beliefs that contradict core biblical teachings

  - *Age Consideration*: More common in later adolescence (16+) as abstract thinking and worldview formation solidify

- **Compartmentalized Faith**: Separating "religious life" from other areas

  - *Age Consideration*: This separation typically increases with age, becoming more pronounced as young people gain independence

- **Abandoning Spiritual Disciplines**: Prayer, Bible reading, worship, and fellowship

  - *Age Consideration*: Look for age-appropriate changes; younger children may need parental initiation of spiritual practices

Social and Relational Changes

- **Dramatic Friendship Changes**: Abandoning positive long-term friendships for concerning new relationships

  - *Age Consideration*: Friend groups naturally shift somewhat during transitions (elementary to middle school, middle to high school), but watch for concerning influences

- **Isolation**: Withdrawing from family and healthy community

  - *Age Consideration*: Some withdrawal from family is normal in adolescence but should be balanced with healthy peer relationships

- **Secretive Communication**: Heightened privacy and defensiveness about online interactions
    - *Age Consideration*: Privacy needs increase naturally with age, but secretiveness combined with mood changes may signal problems
- **Unhealthy Romantic Relationships**: Dating relationships that pull them away from faith values
    - *Age Consideration*: Earlier romantic involvement (before 16) often correlates with higher risk behaviors
- **Conflict Patterns**: Increased family conflict, disrespect toward authority figures
    - *Age Consideration*: Some increase in parent-child conflict is normal during adolescence but should not be persistent or extreme

Digital and Online Behavior

- **Excessive Screen Time**: Interfering with sleep, responsibilities, and in-person relationships
    - *Age Consideration*: Appropriate limits vary by age; children 10-12, especially, need firmer boundaries
- **Content Consumption Shifts**: Interest in harmful, occult, or explicit content
    - *Age Consideration*: Access typically increases with age; monitoring should be higher for younger children
- **Online Persona Changes**: Presenting a drastically different identity online versus offline

   - *Age Consideration*: This risk increases with social media use, which often begins around ages 12-13

- **Digital Isolation**: Using technology to escape rather than connect
   - *Age Consideration*: Look for age-appropriate balance between online and offline activities

- **Harmful Online Communities**: Involvement with groups promoting destructive behaviors
   - *Age Consideration*: These influences may begin earlier than parents expect, sometimes by age 10-11 through gaming platforms

Emotional and Mental Health Indicators

- **Mood Changes**: Persistent sadness, irritability, or emotional numbness
   - *Age Consideration*: Hormonal changes can affect mood, especially ages 11-14, but persistent negative moods warrant attention

- **Anxiety Symptoms**: Excessive worry, panic attacks, avoidance behaviors
   - *Age Consideration*: May present as physical complaints in younger children (stomachaches, headaches)

- **Sleep Disruptions**: Significant changes in sleep patterns
   - *Age Consideration*: Adolescents' biological clocks shift toward later sleep times, but extreme changes remain concerning

- **Substance Use**: Signs of alcohol or drug use as self-medication

- *Age Consideration*: Risk increases throughout adolescence, with initial exposure often occurring between 13-16

Academic and Developmental Concerns

- **Sudden Academic Decline**: Dropping grades, skipping classes, losing motivation
  - *Age Consideration*: Academic transitions (elementary to middle school, middle to high school) may naturally cause temporary adjustment challenges
- **Directionless Drift**: Lack of purpose or direction regarding future
  - *Age Consideration*: More concerning in late high school and beyond; younger children typically have less defined future orientation
- **Extreme Work Patterns**: For older teens, workaholism or inability to maintain employment
  - *Age Consideration*: Primarily relevant for 16+ who have entered the workforce
- **Financial Irresponsibility**: Spending patterns suggesting unhealthy activities
  - *Age Consideration*: Concerning any age, but ability to hide financial behavior increases with age
- **Value Shifts**: Prioritizing material success or social status over character and spiritual growth
  - *Age Consideration*: Values formation is ongoing throughout this developmental period

Physical and Lifestyle Indicators

- **Significant Appearance Changes**: Dramatic shifts potentially indicating identity struggles
    - o *Age Consideration*: Some experimentation is normal, especially ages 13-17; concern increases with extreme changes
- **Substance Abuse Signs**: Physical symptoms, paraphernalia, or behavior changes
    - o *Age Consideration*: While concerning at any age, initial exposure risk often increases around middle school (ages 12-14)
- **Eating Patterns**: Disordered eating behaviors
    - o *Age Consideration*: Risk often increases during puberty (11-14) when body changes occur
- **Risk-Taking Behaviors**: Dangerous activities, legal troubles
    - o *Age Consideration*: Adolescent brain development (continuing into early 20s) affects risk assessment and impulse control
- **Health Neglect**: Abandoning self-care and wellness
    - o *Age Consideration*: Younger children rely more on parents for health routines; increased independence should include appropriate self-care

Words of Encouragement:

If you have just read this chapter and recognized your child in what you read, stop and breathe. The recognition itself is significant. Many parents see the signs and find reasons not to trust what they are seeing. They tell themselves it is a phase, that they are overreacting, that their child is fine. Recognizing warning signs does not mean you have failed as a parent. It means you are paying the kind of attention that Scripture consistently holds up as a virtue. "He who watches over you will not slumber" (Psalm 121:3). God himself is characterized by this watchfulness, and the parent who refuses to look away from what they are seeing in their child is reflecting something of His attentive, protective love.

Do not let that recognition harden into self-condemnation. Warning signs are not proof of parental failure. They are your child communicating something they may not yet have the words or the safety to say directly. The Good Shepherd does not stand at a distance and observe. He goes: "I myself will search for my sheep and look after them. As a shepherd looks after his scattered flock when he is with them, so will I look after my sheep" (Ezekiel 34:11-12). The searching is not a punishment of the sheep for wandering. It is love in motion, love that will not accept distance as the final arrangement.

Jesus asked his followers to be watchful, not with anxiety but with discernment: "Be as shrewd as snakes and as innocent as doves" (Matthew 10:16). That pairing matters. Shrewdness without innocence becomes paranoia. Innocence without shrewdness becomes blindness. The parent this chapter is forming is neither panicked nor naive. They are paying clear-eyed, prayerful attention, the kind that moves when movement is needed. There is a father in the Gospels named Jairus whose daughter was dying. He did not wait at home hoping things would improve. He went to Jesus, fell at his feet, and pleaded with him to come (Mark 5:22-23). That is the posture this chapter is asking of you: not panic, but movement. Not despair, but the willingness to act before the situation demands it.

You will not do this perfectly. There will be moments when you misread a sign, when you respond too quickly or too slowly, when the conversation you initiate goes nowhere. That is part of the work, not evidence that the work is failing. When fear threatens to replace discernment, hold onto this: "God has not given us a spirit of fear, but of power and of love and of a sound mind" (2 Timothy 1:7). That sound mind is available to you. It is the mind that can distinguish a temporary struggle from a persistent pattern, a developmental phase from something requiring action. Ask for it. God gives it. And when you stumble in applying it, remember: "The Lord makes firm the steps of the one who delights in him; though he may stumble, he will not fall, for the Lord upholds him with his hand" (Psalm 37:23-24). You are not being asked to navigate this without stumbling. You are being asked to navigate it without giving up.

Early attention, imperfect and incomplete as it will sometimes be, is still the most powerful intervention available. The prodigal son's father saw him "while he was still a long way off" (Luke 15:20). He was watching. He had kept watching. Your attentiveness today may be the turning point in your child's story tomorrow. And when the concern feels too large, when the pattern you have identified seems beyond what any parent could address, hold onto this: "Nothing is too hard for the Lord" (Jeremiah 32:17). Your child's story is still being written. Keep paying attention. Keep showing up. The Author of that story is not finished with them yet.

5. Biblical Understanding: The Heart Behind Behavior

"Above all else, guard your heart, for everything you do flows from it." (Proverbs 4:23)

When facing concerning behaviors in children and young adults, parents often focus primarily on changing the outward actions. However, a biblical approach recognizes that visible behaviors are merely symptoms of deeper heart issues. This expanded guide explores how understanding your child's heart, their motivations, fears, needs, and beliefs, can lead to more effective and compassionate intervention.

Spiritual Warfare Reality

Scripture reminds us that our children's struggles have spiritual dimensions:

"For we do not wrestle against flesh and blood, but against the rulers, against the authorities, against the cosmic powers over this present darkness, against the spiritual forces of evil in the heavenly places." (Ephesians 6:12)

This biblical perspective acknowledges several important truths:

The Enemy's Strategic Focus

The enemy particularly targets young people during formative years when identity, purpose, and values are being established. These years represent critical spiritual battlegrounds where lifelong patterns are often set.

Beyond Natural Explanations

While not attributing every challenge to direct demonic influence, this perspective reminds us that there are spiritual forces seeking to draw our children away from God's purposes for their lives.

A Balanced Approach

This understanding doesn't dismiss psychological, social, or developmental factors but adds another crucial layer of awareness that helps parents:

- Avoid treating only surface behaviors without addressing spiritual dynamics
- Recognize the need for spiritual tools (prayer, Scripture, community) alongside practical interventions
- Maintain a proper perspective that doesn't view their child as "the enemy" but recognizes external spiritual influences
- Remember the ultimate goal is spiritual formation, not just behavioral compliance

Practical Implications

- **Prayer becomes essential**, not supplemental: "*The prayer of a righteous person is powerful and effective*" (James 5:16)

- **Scriptural application becomes strategic**, addressing spiritual battlegrounds: "*Take the sword of the Spirit, which is the word of God*" (Ephesians 6:17)

- **Community becomes vital**, providing spiritual covering and support: "*Though one may be overpowered, two can defend themselves*" (Ecclesiastes 4:12)

Heart Issues vs. Behavior Modification

"*The good person out of the good treasure of his heart produces good, and the evil person out of his evil treasure produces evil, for out of the abundance of the heart his mouth speaks.*" (Luke 6:45)

Behavior is the fruit, but the heart is the root. Lasting change requires addressing what's happening beneath the surface.

Common Heart Issues in Young People

1. Identity Confusion

- **Heart Need:** To know who they are and that they matter
- **Biblical Truth**: "*You are a chosen people, a royal priesthood, a holy nation, God's special possession*" (1 Peter 2:9)
- **Behavioral Symptoms**: Social media addiction, extreme peer dependence, constant reinvention, unhealthy relationships

2. Need for Belonging

- **Heart Need:** To be accepted and connected
- **Biblical Truth**: "*God sets the lonely in families...*" (Psalm 68:6)
- **Behavioral Symptoms**: People-pleasing, unhealthy friend groups, risky behaviors for acceptance, online community seeking

3. Hunger for Purpose

- **Heart Need:** To know their life has meaning

- **Biblical Truth**: "*For we are God's handiwork, created in Christ Jesus to do good works, which God prepared in advance for us to do*" (Ephesians 2:10)
- **Behavioral Symptoms**: Aimlessness, extreme achievement focus, obsession with causes, nihilistic attitudes

4. Autonomy Without Wisdom

- **Heart Need:** To exercise independence and make choices
- **Biblical Truth**: "*It is for freedom that Christ has set us free*" (Galatians 5:1), balanced with "*The way of fools seems right to them, but the wise listen to advice*" (Proverbs 12:15)
- **Behavioral Symptoms**: Rebellion, risk-taking, rejection of guidance, secret lives

5. Pain Self-Medication

- **Heart Need:** Relief from inner suffering
- **Biblical Truth**: "*He heals the brokenhearted and binds up their wounds*" (Psalm 147:3)
- **Behavioral Symptoms**: Substance use, self-harm, digital escapism, thrill-seeking

FROM THE FIELD

My youngest appeared, by every outward measure, to be the one who handled our international years and our repatriation most gracefully. She was adaptable. She was warm. She found her footing more easily than her siblings, and because she did, I did not look as closely.

What I was not seeing was the weight she was carrying beneath that surface. She was absorbing her brother's pain and her sister's grief and adding it to her own quiet struggles: the pressure to conform to a passport culture she had never truly known, the fishbowl expectation of a ministry child to be perfect and exemplary, the loneliness of building friendships from scratch in a country that felt foreign. All of it carried silently, because she did not want to look weak or need any help from the rest of us.

Behavior tells you something. But it rarely tells you everything. The child who seems fine is sometimes the one who most needs you to look more carefully beneath the surface.

The Limitations of Behavior Modification Alone

Purely behavioral approaches that focus on rules, consequences, and external compliance often fail to create lasting change because they don't address the internal needs and beliefs driving the behavior. While boundaries and consequences have their place, they must be complemented by heart-level intervention.

Why Behavior-Only Approaches Often Fail:

1. **They address symptoms, not causes**
2. **They rely on external control rather than internal motivation**
3. **They can create compliance without heart change**
4. **They often increase rebellion in the long run**
5. **They miss opportunities for deeper spiritual formation**

A More Effective Approach:

1. **Discernment**: Prayerfully seeking to understand what's happening beneath the surface

2. **Conversation**: Asking questions that reveal heart motivations rather than just confronting behaviors

3. **Connection**: Building relationship that creates safety for vulnerable heart discussion

4. **Gospel Application**: Showing how Christ meets the specific heart needs driving the behavior

Common Root Causes of Concerning Behaviors

Understanding potential drivers of concerning behavior helps parents respond with wisdom and compassion.

1. Unresolved Trauma

Past wounds affecting current choices

Biblical Perspective:

- God acknowledges the reality of trauma: "*The brokenhearted*" and "*those who are crushed in spirit*" (Psalm 34:18)

- God promises healing for past wounds: "*I will restore health to you, and your wounds I will heal*" (Jeremiah 30:17)

- Jesus came to "*bind up the brokenhearted*" (Isaiah 61:1)

Parental Response:

- Create safe space to acknowledge painful experiences
- Listen compassionately without minimizing or over-spiritualizing pain
- Connect with appropriate professional help when needed
- Apply biblical truth about God's presence in suffering and power to heal

Signs This Might Be a Factor:

- Extreme reactions to triggers related to past experiences
- Avoidance of certain people, places, or situations
- Recurring nightmares or intrusive thoughts
- Self-protective behaviors that seem excessive

2. Faith Doubts

Intellectual or experiential questions about Christianity

Biblical Perspective:

- Doubt is acknowledged in Scripture: "*Lord, I believe; help my unbelief!*" (Mark 9:24)
- God welcomes honest questions: "*Come now, let us reason together*" (Isaiah 1:18)
- Faith grows through wrestling: Jacob wrestled with God and was blessed (Genesis 32:24-30)

Parental Response:

- Normalize doubts as part of faith development rather than signs of spiritual failure
- Create a safe environment for honest questions without judgment
- Connect with appropriate apologetics resources or mentors
- Share your own journey through doubt with vulnerability

Signs This Might Be a Factor:

- Sudden disinterest in church or spiritual activities
- Asking challenging questions about God, suffering, or biblical reliability
- Interest in other belief systems or atheism
- Statements that suggest faith no longer makes sense

3. Perceived Hypocrisy

Disconnect between professed beliefs and lived reality in Christian community

Biblical Perspective:

- Jesus strongly condemned religious hypocrisy (Matthew 23)

- Scripture distinguishes between imperfect believers and a perfect God
(Romans 3:23-24)

- The church is acknowledged as a community of the redeemed, not the perfect
(1 John 1:8-10)

Parental Response:

- Model authentic faith that acknowledges mistakes
- Distinguish between Christ's perfection and Christian imperfection
- Help process church hurts or disappointments
- Create space for righteous anger while guiding toward forgiveness

Signs This Might Be a Factor:

- Cynical comments about church, Christians, or religious leaders
- Withdrawal after witnessing moral failures in Christian community
- Questions about why Christians don't live what they believe
- Rejection of faith practices while maintaining moral convictions

4. Shame Cycles

Feeling trapped in patterns of sin and unworthiness

Biblical Perspective:

- Shame entered after the Fall (Genesis 3:7-10)
- God provides covering for our shame (Genesis 3:21, symbolically)
- Christ bore our shame on the cross (Hebrews 12:2)
- We are fully accepted in Christ (Ephesians 1:6)

Parental Response:

- Distinguish between conviction (which leads to repentance) and shame (which leads to despair)
- Apply the gospel's message that Christ's righteousness covers our sin
- Break the isolation that shame requires by bringing struggles into the light
- Establish identity based on God's view rather than past failures

Signs This Might Be a Factor:

- Self-destructive behaviors
- Extreme privacy and secrecy
- Resistance to grace or forgiveness
- Language that suggests identity based on failures ("I am bad" vs. "I did something bad")

5. Cultural Pressure

Desire for acceptance from peers and society

Biblical Perspective:

- Scripture warns against conformity to the world (Romans 12:2)
- Jesus acknowledged the cost of following Him in a contrary culture (John 15:19)
- The early church thrived despite cultural opposition (Acts 2:42-47)

Parental Response:

- Recognize the legitimate need for belonging while guiding toward healthier sources
- Equip with biblical worldview to recognize and evaluate cultural messages
- Provide strong Christian community as an alternative source of belonging
- Develop critical thinking skills rather than simply restricting exposure

Signs This Might Be a Factor:

- Increased concern about social status or appearance
- Adopting behaviors or values that conflict with previously held convictions
- Fear of being different or left out
- Parroting cultural talking points without personal reflection

Practical Application: Heart-Focused Intervention

1. Observation: Looking Beyond Behavior

- Watch for patterns that reveal underlying heart issues

- Pay attention to triggers that precede concerning behaviors
- Notice situations where your child thrives versus struggles
- Listen for repeated phrases or themes in conversations

2. Conversation: Heart-Revealing Questions

Questions that help young people articulate their internal motivations:

- "What were you hoping would happen when you...?"
- "What feels most important to you in that situation?"
- "When you feel that way, what do you believe about yourself?"
- "What are you afraid might happen if you didn't...?"
- "What does that experience/relationship give you that you value?"

3. Connection: Building Relational Safety

- Regular time together without agenda
- Sharing appropriately from your own heart struggles
- Responding to vulnerability with grace, not lecture
- Demonstrating unconditional love alongside appropriate boundaries

4. Gospel Application: Addressing Specific Heart Needs

Apply biblical truth to specific heart needs:

- **For identity confusion**: "*You are fearfully and wonderfully made*" (Psalm 139:14)

- **For belonging hunger**: "*God has placed the solitary in families*" (Psalm 68:6)

- **For purpose questions**: "*For we are His workmanship...*" (Ephesians 2:10)

- **For autonomy without wisdom**: "*The fear of the LORD is the beginning of wisdom*" (Proverbs 9:10)

- **For pain self-medication**: "*He heals the brokenhearted...*" (Psalm 147:3)

5. Prayer: Inviting Divine Intervention

- Pray for discernment to see heart issues
- Pray for your child's spiritual eyes to be opened
- Pray for wisdom in your responses
- Pray against spiritual forces targeting your child
- Pray for heart transformation, not just behavior change

Action Steps for Parents

1. **Reflect**: Identify one concerning behavior in your child that you believe might have a deeper heart issue driving it. What might that heart issue be?

2. **Connect**: Set aside time to connect with your child in a low-pressure environment (driving, walking, doing an activity together) where conversation can happen naturally.

3. **Ask**: Use one of the heart-revealing questions from this guide to begin a deeper conversation about what's happening beneath the surface.

4. **Listen**: Practice truly hearing your child's perspective without immediately jumping to correction or solutions.

5. **Pray**: Begin each day by praying specifically for wisdom to see your child's heart needs and for God to work in their heart beyond what your parenting alone can accomplish.

"*I will give you a new heart and put a new spirit in you; I will remove from you your heart of stone and give you a heart of flesh.*" (Ezekiel 36:26)

Words of Encouragement:

The shift this chapter asks of you is one of the most difficult in all of parenting. It is easier to address what you can see. Behavior is visible, measurable, and responsive to consequences. The heart is none of those things. Looking beneath behavior to what is actually driving it requires a kind of discernment that does not come naturally and cannot be manufactured by effort alone.

Scripture is direct about this limitation: "The heart is deceitful above all things and beyond cure. Who can understand it?" (Jeremiah 17:9). The honest answer is that we cannot, not fully, not on our own. But the same passage continues: "I the Lord search the heart and examine the mind" (Jeremiah 17:10). The One who can see into the depths of your child's heart is not you. It is God. Your role is not to achieve a perfect understanding of your child's interior world. It is to stay close enough, and prayerful enough, that God can direct your attention to what actually matters.

Solomon, standing before God at the beginning of his reign, did not ask for wealth or power or long life. He asked for something far more specific: "Give your servant a discerning heart to govern your people and to distinguish between right and wrong" (1 Kings 3:9). That prayer is available to you. The wisdom to see past behavior to the heart beneath it is not something you develop. It is something you receive, from a God who searches hearts and who will give wisdom generously to those who ask (James 1:5).

When you respond to your child with genuine curiosity about what is underneath their behavior, rather than immediate correction of the behavior itself, you are doing something your child may not appreciate in the moment but will not forget. You are communicating that they are more than what they do, that their interior world matters, that you are interested in them rather than simply in managing them. That posture, sustained across years, builds the kind of relationship in which a child eventually tells you the things they have been carrying alone.

Be patient with the slowness of this work. The heart does not change quickly, and the evidence of change is often invisible for a long time. "For the word of God is alive and active. Sharper than any double-edged sword, it penetrates even to dividing soul and spirit... it judges the thoughts and attitudes of the heart" (Hebrews 4:12). God's Word is doing the work you cannot see. Trust it. Keep praying it over your child. The transformation of a heart is God's work, and He does not abandon what He has started.

6. Approaching Difficult Conversations

Creating a Climate of Grace

Before addressing specific concerns:

- **Pray First**: Seek God's wisdom and examine your own heart
- **Choose Timing Wisely**: Find a private moment when everyone is calm
- **Start with Connection**: Begin with affirmation and care, not confrontation
- **Watch Your Nonverbals**: Body language and tone matter as much as words
- **Remember Your Goal**: Restoration and growth, not shame or control

✈ FROM THE FIELD

The full truth about what our son had endured did not surface in a quiet conversation at home. It surfaced in a meeting at his school in Colombia, after a confrontation that forced everything into the open.

A teacher had developed a habit of holding our son up in front of his classmates as an example, not to honor him, but to shame them. Look at this foreigner, he would say, this American, doing better than all of you Colombians. It was a form of bullying with a teacher's authority behind it, and it gave the students both permission and a model. When our son was supposed to submit a group project and one of the students stole his work, the same teacher belittled and humiliated him in front of the class rather than addressing the theft.

We heard about it from other students. We went to the school administrator and filed a complaint. The meeting with the teacher did not go well, but we were there, and we defended our son as we should have. It was in that room, through that conflict, that we finally learned the extent of what had been happening: that the bullying had been systematic, that it was tied directly to his academic success, and that he had been absorbing it alone for far longer than we knew.

Sometimes the difficult conversation is not the one you have with your child. It is the one you have on their behalf, the one where you walk into a room that is not comfortable and refuse to leave until someone is held accountable. Your child may never ask you to do it. Do it anyway.

Age-Appropriate Communication Approaches

For Children 10-13

- **Keep It Simple**: Use concrete language and clear explanations
- **Shorter Conversations**: Attention spans are still developing; multiple shorter talks may be better than one long one
- **Visual Aids**: Drawing, stories, or examples can help clarify complex topics
- **Physical Proximity**: Sitting side-by-side rather than face-to-face may feel less intimidating

- **Reassurance**: Frequently affirm your love and support regardless of the issue
- **Balance**: Maintain appropriate parental authority while still listening well

For Teens 14-17

- **Respect Growing Independence**: Acknowledge their increasing autonomy
- **Avoid Lectures**: Teens respond better to dialogue than monologue
- **Consider Environment**: Some teens talk better during activities (driving, walking) than sitting still
- **Manage Reactions**: Teens may test boundaries with emotional responses; stay calm
- **Digital Options**: Some teens may express themselves better initially through writing or texting about difficult topics
- **Appropriate Vulnerability**: Sharing your own relevant experiences can build connection

For Young Adults 18-24

- **Adult-to-Adult Tone**: Communicate respect for their maturity
- **Collaborative Approach**: Frame conversations as joint problem-solving
- **Acknowledge Changes**: Recognize the evolving parent-child relationship
- **Respect Boundaries**: Honor their increasing privacy and autonomy

- **Invitation vs. Intrusion**: Offer conversation opportunities without demanding them
- **Patience With Process**: Allow more time for reflection and response

Biblical Communication Framework for All Ages

Structure difficult conversations biblically:

- **Listen Before Speaking**: "Let every person be quick to hear, slow to speak, slow to anger" (James 1:19). This means giving your child your full attention without interrupting, formulating responses in your head, or planning your rebuttal while they're still talking. Allow them to complete their thoughts before responding.

- **Ask Questions**: Move from observations to open-ended questions. Open-ended questions cannot be answered with a simple "yes" or "no" but require elaboration and encourage your child to share more deeply. For example, instead of asking "Are you upset?" (closed question), ask "What's been on your mind lately?" or "How have you been feeling about your friendships?" (open-ended questions).

- **Reflect What You Hear**: Validate their perspective even when you disagree. This involves summarizing what your child has said in your own words to show you've understood them, without immediately correcting or judging. For example: "It sounds like you're feeling overwhelmed by the expectations at school and like no one understands what you're going through. Is that right?"

- **Share Your Concern**: Express worry from love, not judgment. Frame your concerns in terms of your care for them rather than disappointment or anger. Compare "I'm concerned about how these choices might affect your future because I love you and want God's best for you" (love-based) with "I can't believe you would do something so irresponsible" (judgment-based).

- **Focus on Impact**: Help them see consequences of choices rather than just imposing rules. Explain how choices affect them and others rather than simply stating what's forbidden. For instance, instead of "You can't stay out past midnight because I said so," try "When you stay out very late, it affects your health through lack of sleep, puts you at higher risk for dangerous situations, and demonstrates to younger siblings that rules aren't important."

- **Offer Support**: Provide practical help for positive change. Move beyond identifying problems to offering specific assistance. This might include: "Would it help if we found a Christian counselor who specializes in these issues?" or "I'm willing to help you practice what to say to your friends if that would be useful" or "Let's work together to create a plan for managing these challenges."

Age-Tailored Conversation Starters

For Children 10-13

- "I noticed you seemed upset after school. Would you like to tell me about your day?"
- "I'm wondering how things are going with your friends lately. Can we talk about that?"
- "I care about what you're feeling. Can you help me understand what's bothering you?"
- "What was the best and hardest part of your day today?"
- "I've noticed [specific change]. Has anything been different for you lately?"

For Teens 14-17

- "I've noticed [observation] and I'm wondering what's been going on for you lately."
- "I care about you deeply, which is why I wanted to check in about [specific concern]."
- "Help me understand more about [situation/behavior/choice] from your perspective."
- "What's been on your mind lately that you might want to talk about?"
- "I'm concerned about [behavior], not because I want to control you, but because I love you. Can we talk about it?"

For Young Adults 18-24

- "I've noticed [observation] and wanted to check in. Would you be open to talking about it?"
- "I respect that you're making your own decisions. I'm here if you want to process anything together."
- "What would be helpful for you right now in terms of support?"
- "I'm concerned about how [behavior] might be affecting your wellbeing and future. Would you be willing to share your perspective?"
- "I value our relationship and want to understand what you're experiencing. Can we talk more about this?"

Words of Encouragement:

Every difficult conversation you initiate is an invaluable investment in your relationship with your child, reflecting how God engages with us. Throughout Scripture, we see God's willingness to tackle challenging conversations with those He loves. From His poignant question to Adam in the garden, "Where are you?" (Genesis 3:9), to His patient exchanges with Job, and Jesus' heartfelt discussions with His disciples, these moments show us the importance of honest dialogue.

God's Word reminds us that "reckless words pierce like swords, but the tongue of the wise brings healing" (Proverbs 12:18). When conversations get uncomfortable or don't unfold as you hoped, remember that Jesus was described as "full of grace and truth" (John 1:14), perfectly balancing loving acceptance with straightforward communication. Your courage to have these discussions demonstrates that nothing can sever your child's connection to your love, mirroring the unconditional love of the Father.

As you gear up for these conversations, take comfort in the promise that God offers wisdom generously when we ask: "If any of you lacks wisdom, you should ask God" (James 1:5). The Holy Spirit is right there with you, interceding "with groans that words cannot express" (Romans 8:26), guiding your words and softening your child's heart. Even when it feels tough to find the right words, know that God is "able to do immeasurably more than all we ask or imagine" (Ephesians 3:20).

Your willingness to tackle tough topics teaches your child that no subject is too difficult, and no struggle too shameful to bring into the light. Remember, "the truth will set you free" (John 8:32). The courage you display in these conversations builds bridges that your child can cross in their moments of greatest need.

Think of King David's story, where confrontation became a path to repentance and restoration through Nathan's words (2 Samuel 12). Your conversations may not always yield immediate results, but take heart in Isaiah's assurance that God's word "will not return to me empty" (Isaiah

55:11). Trust that God is working in the spaces between your words, fostering insight and connection beyond what you can see in the moment. These challenging conversations fulfill the command to "speak the truth in love" (Ephesians 4:15) and plant seeds that can bear fruit in your child's life for years to come, equipping them to communicate honestly and graciously about difficult matters.

7. Biblical Intervention Strategies

Balancing Grace and Truth

Jesus came "full of grace and truth" (John 1:14). Both elements are essential in parenting children and young adults of all ages:

- **Grace Without Truth**: Permissiveness that fails to protect, "*Whoever spares the rod hates their children, but the one who loves their children is careful to discipline them.*" (Proverbs 13:24)

A note on the rod: Proverbs 13:24 has historically been used to justify physical discipline of children. The intent of biblical discipline is the formation of character and the protection of the child's wellbeing, not the infliction of physical pain. Research consistently demonstrates that physical punishment produces more harm than benefit, contributing to increased aggression, behavioral problems, diminished mental health, and damaged parent-child relationships. Evidence-based, non-physical forms of discipline, including natural consequences, logical consequences, privilege adjustment, and collaborative problem-solving, achieve the outcomes this scripture is pointing toward without the documented risks. Regardless of cultural context, parents are encouraged to pursue discipline methods that keep both the child's body and the parent-child relationship fully intact.

- **Truth Without Grace**: Legalism that damages relationship, "*Fathers, do not exasperate your children; instead, bring them up in the training and instruction of the Lord.*" (Ephesians 6:4)

- **Grace and Truth Together**: Loving guidance that promotes growth, "*Teach me knowledge and good judgment, for I trust your commands.*" (Psalm 119:66)

Setting Biblical Boundaries Across Developmental Stages

Healthy boundaries reflect God's character while acknowledging developmental needs:

For Children 10-13

- **Clear, Simple Expectations**: Straightforward rules with specific guidance, "*Let me understand the teaching of your precepts; then I will meditate on your wonders.*" (Psalm 119:27)

- **Regular Supervision**: Closer monitoring of activities and digital life, "*My eyes are always on the LORD, for he rescues my feet from the snare.*" (Psalm 25:15)

- **Structured Environment**: Maintaining routine and predictability, "*But everything should be done in a fitting and orderly way.*" (1 Corinthians 14:40)

- **Immediate Consequences**: Timely, appropriate responses to boundary violations, "*Discipline your children, for in that there is hope; do not be a willing party to their death.*" (Proverbs 19:18)

- **Emphasis on Safety**: Clear focus on physical and emotional wellbeing, "*Guard your heart above all else, for it determines the course of your life.*" (Proverbs 4:23, NLT)

- **Guided Decision-Making**: Teaching decision skills through scaffolded choices, "*I will instruct you and teach you in the way you should go; I will counsel you with my loving eye on you.*" (Psalm 32:8)

For Teens 14-17

- **Collaborative Boundaries**: Increasing teen input while maintaining parental authority, "*Plans fail for lack of counsel, but with many advisers they succeed.*" (Proverbs 15:22)

- **Graduated Freedoms**: Expanding independence based on demonstrated responsibility, "*Whoever can be trusted with very little can also be trusted with much.*" (Luke 16:10)

- **Critical Thinking Development**: "Why" behind boundaries, not just "what", "*Come now, let us reason together, says the LORD.*" (Isaiah 1:18, ESV)

- **Natural Consequences**: Allowing them to experience appropriate results of choices, "*A person reaps what they sow.*" (Galatians 6:7)

- **Renegotiation Process**: Periodic reassessment of boundaries as maturity increases, "*When I was a child, I talked like a child, I thought like a child, I reasoned like a child. When I became a man, I put the ways of childhood behind me.*" (1 Corinthians 13:11)

- **Digital Boundaries**: Clear technology agreements with monitoring appropriate to age, "*I will set no worthless thing before my eyes.*" (Psalm 101:3, NASB)

For Young Adults 18-24

- **Advisory Role**: Shifting from control to influence and counsel, "*Listen to advice and accept discipline, and at the end you will be counted among the wise.*" (Proverbs 19:20)

- **Respect for Autonomy**: Acknowledging their legal adult status, "*It is for freedom that Christ has set us free.*" (Galatians 5:1)

- **Living Arrangement Clarity**: Clear expectations for those living at home, "*Anyone who does not provide for their relatives, and especially for their own household, has denied the faith and is worse than an unbeliever.*" (1 Timothy 5:8)

- **Financial Boundaries**: Transparent agreements about economic support, "*The borrower is slave to the lender.*" (Proverbs 22:7)

- **Invitation vs. Intrusion**: Offering guidance without demanding compliance, "*Let your conversation be always full of grace, seasoned with salt, so that you may know how to answer everyone.*" (Colossians 4:6)

- **Relationship Consequences**: Focus on relational impact rather than imposed penalties, "*If your brother or sister sins, go and point out their fault, just between the two of you.*" (Matthew 18:15)

FROM THE FIELD

I grew up in a home where 'why' was not a welcome question. You did what you were told, you obeyed without asking, and if you pushed back you met the consequences. A short time in the military reinforced the same thing: obey orders, follow commands, don't question the chain. That formation went deep, and it followed me into fatherhood.

I tried to be different with my children. I genuinely tried to explain my reasoning, to help them understand rather than simply comply. But when one of them asked why, really pressed into it, I did not always respond with patience. I sometimes

> *heard the question as a challenge to my authority rather than what it actually was: a child trying to understand the world and their place in it.*
>
> *The irony is that the 'why' question is not defiance. It is engagement. A child who asks why is a child who is thinking, who wants to be included in the reasoning, who is building the internal framework they will eventually use to make decisions on their own. Shutting it down doesn't produce obedience; it produces compliance without understanding, which is the last thing you want when they are old enough to make their own choices, and you are no longer in the room.*

Practical Accountability Systems by Age

Implement age-appropriate structures to support positive change:

For Children 10-13

- **Parent-Led Check-ins**: Regular conversations initiated by parents, "*These commandments that I give you today are to be on your hearts. Impress them on your children. Talk about them when you sit at home and when you walk along the road, when you lie down and when you get up.*" (Deuteronomy 6:6-7)
- **Visible Monitoring**: Open and clear oversight of activities and technology, "*The eye of the LORD is on those who fear him, on those who hope in his steadfast love.*" (Psalm 33:18, ESV)
- **Family Participation**: Involvement in family devotions and activities, "*But as for me and my household, we will serve the LORD.*" (Joshua 24:15)

- **Appropriate Mentors**: Supervised relationships with other trusted adults, "*Get wisdom, get understanding; do not forget my words or turn away from them.*" (Proverbs 4:5)

- **Skill Building**: Teaching self-regulation and healthy habit formation, "*Train up a child in the way he should go; even when he is old he will not depart from it.*" (Proverbs 22:6, ESV)

For Teens 14-17

- **Mentorship**: Connect them with trusted adults beyond parents, "*Walk with the wise and become wise, for a companion of fools suffers harm.*" (Proverbs 13:20)

- **Healthy Peer Groups**: Facilitate involvement with positive friend groups, "*Do not be misled: 'Bad company corrupts good character.'*" (1 Corinthians 15:33)

- **Regular Check-ins**: Consistent communication with increasing depth, "*Open my eyes that I may see wonderful things in your law.*" (Psalm 119:18)

- **Technology Management**: Appropriate monitoring while teaching discernment, "*Test everything. Hold on to what is good. Avoid every kind of evil.*" (1 Thessalonians 5:21-22, NIV 1984)

- **Spiritual Accountability**: Connection with youth groups and student ministries, "*And let us consider how we may spur one another on toward love and good deeds, not giving up meeting together.*" (Hebrews 10:24-25)

For Young Adults 18-24

- **Adult Mentoring Relationships**: Facilitating connections with mature believers, *"Follow my example, as I follow the example of Christ."* (1 Corinthians 11:1)

- **Peer Community**: Encouraging involvement in young adult ministries or groups, *"Iron sharpens iron, and one man sharpens another."* (Proverbs 27:17, ESV)

- **Mutual Respect**: Accountability based on relationship rather than authority, *"Be devoted to one another in love. Honor one another above yourselves."* (Romans 12:10)

- **Resource Provision**: Offering tools and support while respecting autonomy, *"And my God will meet all your needs according to the riches of his glory in Christ Jesus."* (Philippians 4:19)

- **Professional Connections**: Helping access appropriate professional support when needed, *"Without good guidance, people fall, but with many advisors there is safety."* (Proverbs 11:14, NET)

A Plan B Approach: Collaborative Problem Solving

When standard approaches to boundaries and consequences are not producing results, Collaborative Problem Solving offers a different framework. Rather than imposing solutions from the top down, this approach involves the parent and child working together to identify what is making a situation difficult and developing a solution that addresses both the parent's concern and the child's. This does not mean abandoning parental authority. It means bringing the child into the problem-solving process in a way that builds their capacity to manage conflict, develop empathy, and practice decision-making.

The basic approach involves three steps. First, the parent approaches the child with genuine curiosity about what is making the situation difficult for them, listening without immediately problem-solving or defending the rule. Second, the parent shares their own underlying concern, not the rule itself but the reason the rule matters. Third, the parent and child work together to generate solutions that address both concerns.

This approach is particularly effective with children who are emotionally dysregulated, persistently oppositional, or who have not responded well to consequence-based discipline. It is also consistent with a foundational principle of this resource: children who are struggling are almost always communicating something. The goal of discipline is not compliance. It is growth.

Not all professional help looks the same, and knowing who to call and when can make a meaningful difference in how effectively your child receives the support they need.

A school counselor is typically available through your child's school and can provide support for academic concerns, social difficulties, and mild emotional challenges. School counselors are not licensed mental health clinicians and are generally not equipped to provide ongoing therapy or address significant mental health conditions. They are, however, an accessible first point of contact and can often provide referrals to appropriate resources.

A licensed therapist or psychologist is a trained mental health professional who provides ongoing clinical support for behavioral, emotional, and relational concerns. If your child is experiencing persistent anxiety, depression, trauma responses, significant behavioral changes, or struggles that are affecting daily functioning, a licensed therapist is the appropriate level of care. When possible, seek a therapist who has experience working with adolescents and whose approach is compatible with your family's faith values.

An emergency room visit or a call to 988, the Suicide and Crisis Lifeline, is the appropriate response when your child is in acute danger. This includes expressing active suicidal intent, engaging in serious self-harm, experiencing a mental health crisis that you cannot safely manage at home, or appearing to be at immediate risk of harming themselves or others. In these situations, do not wait for a scheduled appointment. Go directly to your nearest emergency room or call 988 for immediate guidance.

When to Seek Additional Help

Recognize when issues exceed typical parenting challenges, with age-specific considerations:

For All Ages

- **Signs of Crisis**: Suicidal thoughts, severe substance abuse, self-harm, "*Bear one another's burdens, and so fulfill the law of Christ.*" (Galatians 6:2, ESV)

- **Persistent Patterns**: Issues continuing despite consistent intervention, "*Is there no balm in Gilead? Is there no physician there? Why then is there no healing for the wound of my people?*" (Jeremiah 8:22)

- **Impact Severity**: Behaviors threatening health, safety, or long-term wellbeing, "*For I know the plans I have for you, declares the LORD, plans for welfare and not for evil, to give you a future and a hope.*" (Jeremiah 29:11, ESV)

- **Resource Needs**: Situations requiring specialized knowledge or support, "*Where there is no guidance, a people falls, but in an abundance of counselors there is safety.*" (Proverbs 11:14, ESV)

- **Parental Burnout**: When you need support to continue effective parenting, "*Come to me, all you who are weary and burdened, and I will give you rest.*" (Matthew 11:28)

Additional Considerations by Age

- **Ages 10-13**: Significant developmental regressions, extreme mood changes, school refusal, "*He tends his flock like a shepherd: He gathers the lambs in his arms and carries them close to his heart; he gently leads those that have young.*" (Isaiah 40:11)

- **Ages 14-17**: Dangerous risk-taking, severe family conflict, serious academic decline, social isolation, "*My son, do not despise the LORD's discipline, and do not resent his rebuke, because the LORD disciplines those he loves, as a father the son he delights in.*" (Proverbs 3:11-12)

- **Ages 18-24**: Inability to function independently, destructive lifestyle patterns, rejection of previously embraced values, "*Even though I walk through the darkest valley, I will fear no evil, for you are with me; your rod and your staff, they comfort me.*" (Psalm 23:4)

Words of Encouragement:

Setting biblical boundaries is not about control, it's about cultivating a nurturing environment where your child can thrive. Just as God establishes loving boundaries for His children, you too can create a space that promotes growth and security. The psalmist beautifully expressed this when he wrote, "The boundary lines have fallen for me in pleasant places" (Psalm 16:6). By balancing grace with truth in your parenting, you reflect God's heart to your child. Remember, Moses reminded Israel that God's rules were "for your own good" (Deuteronomy 10:13). This illustrates that true boundaries stem from love, not a desire to control.

Your steady guidance provides the security your child needs in a world that can feel chaotic and directionless. The Bible wisely states, "In the paths of the wicked are snares and pitfalls, but those who would preserve their life stay far from them" (Proverbs 22:5). The limits you establish today are not walls that confine your child; they are channels that guide them toward a healthy, fulfilling life.

Taking action when your child is at risk can be daunting and may come with its share of resistance. Yet, hold onto the promise that good results are on the horizon: "No discipline seems pleasant at the time, but painful. Later on, it produces a harvest of righteousness and peace" (Hebrews 12:11). Your child might push back against boundaries now, but many children later express gratitude for the loving limits their parents set. Just as King Hezekiah "did what was good and right" by removing harmful idols from his land (2 Chronicles 31:20), your courage to confront destructive influences paves the way for your child's spiritual growth.

When you encounter resistance, remember the wisdom of Mordecai, who told Esther, "Who knows but that you have come to your position for such a time as this?" (Esther 4:14). God has placed you in this role, equipped with unique insight and love, to support your child during this critical time.

Your calling as a parent is a sacred trust. God is working through your loving guidance in ways you may not yet see. He promises, "My word...will not return to me empty, but will achieve the purpose for which I sent it" (Isaiah 55:11). When change feels slow, take heart in these words: "For the revelation awaits an appointed time... Though it linger, wait for it; it will certainly come" (Habakkuk 2:3). The care and limits you provide, even when progress seems hidden, lay a foundation that can support your child for a lifetime. As you implement these strategies, claim this promise: "Not by might, nor by power, but by my Spirit, says the LORD" (Zechariah 4:6). Your efforts, fueled by God's Spirit rather than solely your own strength, become powerful channels for His transformative work in your child's life.

8. Digital Life, Substances, and At-Risk Behaviors

"Do not conform to the pattern of this world, but be transformed by the renewing of your mind." (Romans 12:2)

Every generation of parents has faced a version of this challenge. Television. Video games. The internet. Each new technology arrived with promises and problems, and each generation of parents had to decide, often without a roadmap, how to steward their child's access to it. What is different today is not the presence of technology in a child's life. It is the combination of portability, anonymity, algorithmic design, and social comparison that makes the current landscape genuinely different from anything that came before it.

The chapters ahead are not about making your child's life technology-free. That is neither possible nor wise. Children who grow up without digital fluency will be unprepared for the world they are entering. The goal is not elimination. It is formation, establishing the values, habits, and identity in your child early enough that those things travel with them even when your direct supervision does not.

The same principle applies to substances, and risk behaviors. The parent who waits until their teenager is in trouble to begin the conversation has started too late. The most powerful protection you can give your child against external pressures is not a rule. It is a relationship, a formed identity, and a home culture that speaks louder than the culture outside it.

These are the challenges coming at your child from the outside. Your job is to be present in your child's world long before those challenges arrive, so that when they do, your voice is already the loudest one in the room.

Digital Life and Social Media

Platforms built for profit are not designed around your child's wellbeing. They are designed to maximize engagement, which means they are designed to hold your child's attention as long as possible, serving content that provokes the strongest emotional response. Outrage, comparison, desire, and fear are more engaging than contentment. That is not an accident. It is the business model.

Social media specifically creates conditions that are uniquely hostile to adolescent development. The years between ten and twenty-four are precisely the years when identity is being formed, when peer acceptance feels life-or-death, when the brain is still developing its capacity for impulse control and long-term thinking. Social media is designed to exploit all three of those vulnerabilities simultaneously. Understanding this is not cause for panic. It is cause for intentionality.

The parent who establishes a digital culture in the home before their child has a smartphone is building a foundation. The parent who waits until problems emerge is doing damage control. Both are better than doing nothing, but the first is far more effective.

Guidance by Age

Ages 10-13: This is the most critical window for establishing digital habits that will carry into adolescence. Children in this age range are being introduced to devices, platforms, and online communities at an age when their capacity for self-regulation is still developing. Parents should position themselves as active participants in their child's digital life, not monitors from a distance. Know what your child is watching and playing. Sit with them. Ask questions about what they enjoy and why. Establish clear, consistent time limits and enforce them calmly and consistently. Devices belong in common areas of the home during these years. The bedroom is not yet the right environment for unsupervised screen access.

Ages 14-17: Teenagers will push against digital limits, and some degree of that push is developmentally appropriate. The goal in these years is not tighter control but deeper conversation. Why does this platform make you feel the way it does? What are you looking for when you open that app? Help your teenager develop the language to examine their own digital habits. Continue to maintain clear household agreements about time, platforms, and privacy, while gradually expanding freedom as responsibility is demonstrated. Social media in these years deserves specific, honest conversation about comparison, self-image, and the gap between what people post and how they actually live.

Ages 18-24: Young adults making their own digital choices are beyond parental enforcement, but not beyond parental influence. The habits and values established in the earlier years are the primary protection now. Stay engaged with your young adult's life without monitoring their accounts. Ask how they are managing their relationship with technology. Model healthy habits yourself. If you notice patterns of digital isolation, compulsive use, or significant mood changes connected to social media, name what you are observing and offer to talk about it. Your voice still matters even when your authority has rightly diminished.

FROM THE FIELD

When our son was very young, we made a deliberate decision: no cable television. Our children grew up on Veggie Tales and age-appropriate videos, and when tablets entered the home, they came loaded with learning games only. Leap Frog Reading. Educational content. Nothing else. As they got older, usage was time-limited and monitored consistently. Our children did not receive cell phones until after they were sixteen.

My youngest found a creative workaround. She convinced her brother to buy her one. We took it away.

It would be dishonest to suggest this was easy or that our children complied without resistance. It was a constant battle across many years. There were moments of frustration on all sides. But today, all three of my children are well-disciplined in their relationship with technology. My son is an avid reader who would rather have a book in his hand than a screen in front of him. The fight was worth it, and it was worth it precisely because we started it early, held the line consistently, and stayed present in the battle even when it was exhausting.

The digital boundary you set today is not a wall. It is a foundation. The values you establish in those early years travel with your child long after you are no longer in the room to enforce them.

Substance Use and Risk Behaviors

Risk behaviors rarely begin with a dramatic choice. They begin with small compromises, with curiosity that has no healthy outlet, with pain that has no name yet, with peer pressure that feels manageable in the moment. By the time a parent recognizes that something has changed, the pattern is often already well established.

What the research consistently shows is that the most effective protection against substance use is not primarily a rule or a consequence. It is the quality of the relationship between parent and child, the strength of the child's sense of identity and belonging, and the presence of a community that grounds them in something larger than the moment. Children who know who they are, who have a family that has spoken identity and worth over them consistently, are statistically less vulnerable to the draw of substances as a coping mechanism. This does not make them immune. But it gives them a place to stand.

Parents should also resist the instinct to assume their child will be the exception. Exposure to substances typically begins earlier than parents expect, and it frequently begins in environments that parents consider safe. Churches, sports teams, close friend groups. The conversation about substances is not one conversation. It is a recurring, evolving dialogue that begins before exposure and continues through young adulthood.

Guidance by Age

Ages 10-13: Prevention in these years is about building protective factors before exposure occurs. Help your child develop a strong, internalized sense of identity, the kind that does not depend on peer approval. Teach them explicitly about the physical and emotional effects of substances in age-appropriate language, without dramatizing or minimizing. Role-play peer pressure scenarios with them so they have practiced language for saying no before they need it. Create a home environment where they know they can tell you hard things without being met with explosive reactions. That safety will matter enormously in a few years.

Ages 14-17: This is the period of highest exposure risk for most young people. Adolescent brain development, specifically the gap between the emotional brain and the still-developing prefrontal cortex, makes teenagers genuinely more susceptible to impulsive decisions than adults. They are not simply being foolish. Their brains are wired for novelty and risk at exactly the age when substances are most available. Honest, specific conversations about substances work better than lectures. Ask what they are seeing in their social environment. Listen without immediately correcting. Address the underlying needs that substances often attempt to meet: belonging, relief from stress, escape from pain. Help them find those things through healthier channels.

Ages 18-24: Young adults making independent choices about substances require a different approach. Direct parental control is no longer the lever. Relationship is. If you have maintained an honest, non-reactive relationship through the earlier years, you have access that matters now. Share your concern clearly and once, without repeated pressure. Connect them with recovery resources if patterns have become concerning. Never let the topic become the only thing you talk about. The relationship itself is the most powerful intervention available at this stage.

Words of Encouragement:

The culture your child is growing up in is not neutral. It is engineered, deliberately and expertly, to capture attention and hold it. The platforms, the algorithms, the content streams, they are designed by teams of people whose professional purpose is to make your child want to keep scrolling, keep watching, keep coming back. And those same forces are competing for your attention too. You are not parenting in a vacuum. You are parenting in an environment that is working against you and against your child simultaneously, and doing so with resources and sophistication that no individual family can match.

That is the honest reality. And it matters because the parent who does not name it will eventually wonder why the fight feels so relentless. It feels relentless because it is relentless. You are not failing. You are fighting something that does not rest, does not relent, and does not care about your child the way you do. Naming that clearly is not cause for despair. It is cause for the kind of deliberate, consistent, long-view parenting that this chapter is asking of you.

We live in a culture of immediate results. We expect fast answers, fast delivery, fast resolution. That expectation seeps into parenting without us noticing it, and it produces a specific kind of discouragement: the sense that if we are not seeing results now, what we are doing is not working. But the formation of a child does not operate on that timeline. It never has. The parent who cancels the cable channels when their child is three will not see the payoff when the child is four. They may not see it when the child is fourteen. They may only see it when their adult child, sitting across from them years later, makes a choice that reflects the values that were spoken over them before they were old enough to understand what values were.

Scripture has always understood this. The farmer who plants does not stand over the ground demanding to see the harvest by morning. He prepares the soil, he plants the seed, he tends what he has planted, and then he waits. "He who goes out weeping, carrying seed to sow, will return with songs of joy, carrying sheaves with him" (Psalm 126:6). The weeping is real. The seed is real. And so is the harvest, even when it is not yet visible.

Consider also that the God who set the boundaries of the sea (Job 38:11), who established limits not to confine creation but to protect it, is the same God working alongside you as you set limits in your home. Your boundaries are not arbitrary. They are an act of love that reflects the character of a God who has always understood that protection and freedom are not opposites. They are a parent and a child. The limit is what makes the freedom possible.

So when the fight feels exhausting, when your child pushes back for the hundredth time and the culture offers them a hundred and one reasons why you are wrong, hold onto this: you are not fighting alone, and you are not fighting on a short timeline. "Let us not become weary in doing good, for at the proper time we will reap a harvest if we do not give up" (Galatians 6:9). The proper time is not your time. It is God's. And in His economy, nothing you have faithfully planted in your child's life is ever wasted.

9. Faith, Identity, and Sexuality

"Before I formed you in the womb I knew you, before you were born I set you apart." (Jeremiah 1:5)

The questions in this chapter are not coming at your child from outside. They are rising from within. Who am I? What do I actually believe, not what my family believes, but what I believe? How do I understand my body, my desires, my place in the world? These are not questions that appear suddenly in adolescence and disappear in adulthood. They are the questions of a lifetime, and the answers a young person arrives at during the years between ten and twenty-four will shape the trajectory of everything that follows.

Parents who try to shut these questions down, do not eliminate them. They simply ensure their child works through them alone, without the guidance, the perspective, or the love that a parent could have offered. The goal is not to prevent the questions. It is to be present when they come.

This chapter is about the questions your child is working out from the inside. That means your role here is less about intervention and more about formation, less about correction and more about conversation. It requires more patience than the previous chapter, more tolerance for ambiguity, and more willingness to sit with your child in uncertainty without immediately reaching for resolution. The parent who can do that will have access to their child's inner world in ways that matter enormously.

Faith Struggles and Doubts

Faith that has never been questioned is not yet fully the child's own. Every young person raised in a Christian home must, at some point, determine whether what they believe is genuinely theirs or simply the air their family breathes. This is not a spiritual crisis. It is a developmental inevitability, and it is a sign that your child is taking faith seriously enough to examine it.

The parent's role in this season is not to defend God. God does not need defending, and a parent who responds to their child's questions with anxiety or pressure communicates that the questions themselves are dangerous. They are not. They are the beginning of an examined faith, which is the only kind that holds through the actual trials of adult life.

What your child needs from you during a season of faith struggle is first your honesty, then your presence, and then your patience. Honesty means acknowledging that you have had your own questions. Presence means staying in the conversation rather than shutting it down. Patience means trusting that God is at work in the wrestling, even when you cannot see it.

Guidance by Age

Ages 10-13: Children in this age range are beginning to move from inherited faith toward a more personal understanding. Questions at this stage are often concrete: Why does God let bad things happen? How do we know the Bible is true? These are not attacks on faith. They are invitations to think together. Answer honestly, explore together, and resist the temptation to shut the conversation down with a pat answer. A child who learns that questions are welcome at home will bring their bigger questions home in the years ahead.

Ages 14-17: Teenagers may express doubt more forcefully, sometimes with apparent contempt for faith they once embraced. This intensity is rarely about theology. It is almost always about identity, belonging, or pain. Before engaging the intellectual content of your teenager's doubt, ask what is underneath it. What happened? What does it feel like to not be sure? The questions are the doorway to the conversation that actually matters. Introduce thoughtful apologetics resources, connect them with mentors and youth communities that take hard questions seriously, and share your own faith journey with appropriate vulnerability. A parent who has wrestled with belief has far more to offer a wrestling teenager than one who presents only certainty.

Ages 18-24: Young adults in this season may be processing faith questions in college, in new communities, or in silence. The parent's role shifts here to respectful, adult-to-adult conversation. Engage with their actual questions at a serious intellectual level. Resist the urge to lecture or to treat their doubt as a parenting failure. Connect them with thoughtful communities of faith where questions are welcome. And pray, consistently and specifically, for the faith that took root in them to find its own expression. Faith found in the hard places, as many parents have witnessed in their own children, is the kind that no one can give and no one can take away.

FROM THE FIELD

My oldest daughter had a rebellious season in her early teens, strong-willed, questioning, pushing against everything. My wife, at a point of both wisdom and perhaps exhaustion, told her that if she was going to question things, she should start with the Bible. So she did.

She started in Genesis and read straight through. I walked in on her one afternoon reading aloud from a passage in the Old Testament that was, to put it plainly, not what I expected a young teenager to be working through on her own. I asked her what she was reading. She looked up and said simply: the Bible. Then she proceeded to tell me everything she had been learning.

She went through some very hard seasons. There were times, I believe, when she wondered whether God had abandoned her, whether the faith she had grown up with was actually real or simply the air her family breathed. But she came out the other side with something no one could give her and no one could take from her. She reminds me now, when the weight of things gets heavy, that God said He will never leave us nor forsake us. She didn't inherit that conviction from us. She found it herself, in the hard places. That is the only kind of faith that holds.

Identity Formation

Identity is not something a child discovers on their own. It is something that is formed, word by word and year by year, by the voices that speak into their life most consistently and most authoritatively. A child's identity will be shaped by something. The question is whether the parent will be intentional about shaping it first, or whether the culture, the peer group, and the algorithm will do it instead.

This is especially urgent in the years before major transitions, before adolescence, before an international move, before a new school, before any season when the outside world will press hard against a child's sense of self. The child who knows who they are before the world asks the question has a place to stand when the answer is challenged. The child who does not know has nothing to hold onto.

Biblical identity is not a feeling. It is a declaration. You are known before you were formed (Jeremiah 1:5). You are wonderfully made (Psalm 139:14). You are loved with an everlasting love (Jeremiah 31:3). You belong to God. These truths do not become real to a child because a parent says them once. They become real because a parent says them again and again, in ordinary moments and in hard ones, until the child has heard them enough times that the voice they hear in their own head begins to sound like truth.

Guidance by Age

Ages 10-13: This is the window for establishing the foundational declarations of identity that will anchor your child through the turbulence of adolescence. Speak specifically and consistently over your child: who they are, whose they are, what they carry, what they are made for. Family identity matters here as well as spiritual identity. A child who knows they belong to something, a family with shared values, a tradition, a name, has a stronger foundation than one who is left to construct identity entirely from peer feedback. Begin the conversation about identity in Christ early and revisit it often.

Ages 14-17: Adolescence is the season when identity formation is most active and most vulnerable to outside influence. Peers, social media, romantic relationships, and cultural messaging are all competing to define your teenager before you can. Your job is not to eliminate those voices but to be louder and more consistent. Continue to speak identity over your teenager even when they resist it, and especially when they resist it. Engage in specific conversations about what they believe about themselves, what the culture is telling them, and what Scripture says in response. Help them develop the capacity to examine the messages coming at them rather than simply absorbing them.

Ages 18-24: Young adults are consolidating the identity that has been forming across the previous decade. The parent's role now is to affirm and support rather than to direct. Continue to speak truth over them. Celebrate who they are becoming. If they are carrying distorted beliefs about themselves, whether from past wounds, cultural messaging, or seasons of failure, address those gently and specifically with the truth of who God says they are. The investment of speaking identity consistently in the earlier years pays its most visible dividend here, when the young adult who knows who they are can navigate the complexity of early adulthood from a stable foundation.

FROM THE FIELD

From the time my son was five or six years old, I began speaking the same words over my children, consistently and deliberately: we are Roddys. We are different. We are Christian first. We give a hundred and ten percent and we never give up.

As we prepared for international ministry and the reality of raising our children across cultures and countries became clear, I said it more often and with more intention. I wanted to make sure my children knew exactly who they were before the world had a chance to tell them differently. You are American. You are not Mexican, not Colombian, not Peruvian. You are a child of God, wonderfully and beautifully made in His image. That is who you are, and no country, no culture, and no classroom can change it.

Today, all three of my children are patriotic, grounded, and clear about who they are. They know to whom they belong. That did not happen by accident. It happened because we spoke it over them before the world got there first.

Identity is not something your child will simply discover on their own. It is something you help form, word by word, year by year, long before they are old enough to know they needed it.

Sexuality and Peer Relationships

The conversation about sexuality is not one conversation. It is a hundred smaller conversations across a decade, each one calibrated to the child's age and readiness, each one adding a piece to a framework that should be largely in place before the larger questions arrive. Parents who wait until adolescence to begin this conversation are starting late. Parents who never begin it leave their child to construct a sexual ethic entirely from cultural sources, which are neither reliable nor biblically grounded.

Biblical sexuality is not primarily a list of prohibitions. It is a positive vision of what human beings are made for: relationship, intimacy, covenant, and the image of God reflected in the union of persons made in His likeness. That positive vision is far more compelling than a rulebook, and far more sustainable through the years when temptation is real and the cultural pressure is significant.

Parents should also approach the topic of peer and romantic relationships with the same intentionality. The friendships and romantic relationships your child forms during these years are not peripheral to their development. They are formative. The peers your child spends the most time with will shape their values, their habits, and their sense of what is normal. Investing in your child's relational world is not intrusive. It is essential.

Guidance by Age

Ages 10-13: Begin with the body, honestly and simply, in age-appropriate language. Children who receive accurate information about puberty and development from their parents are better equipped to process what they experience and less susceptible to misinformation from peers. Establish the framework of biblical identity as the foundation for all conversations about sexuality: your body is made by God, it is good, it belongs to Him, and how you treat it matters. Create a home environment where questions about bodies, relationships, and attraction can be asked without shame.

Ages 14-17: Teenagers are navigating the intersection of biological development, social pressure, romantic interest, and cultural messaging about sex and gender simultaneously. The parent who has established open conversation in the earlier years has access to this season that the parent who waited does not. Engage specifically and honestly with the questions your teenager is actually asking, not only the ones you are comfortable with. Help them understand the difference between attraction and action, between feelings and choices. Teach the biblical vision of relationships as covenant rather than consumption. Address the specific cultural messages they are encountering about gender and sexuality with both conviction and compassion.

Ages 18-24: Young adults are making independent choices about relationships, physical intimacy, and sexual ethics. The parent's role is to maintain relationship and influence, not control. Continue to speak the biblical vision clearly and without apology, while extending the grace that makes continued conversation possible. If your young adult is making choices you disagree with, address it once with clarity and love, and then maintain the relationship. A parent who cuts off connection over sexual ethics loses all further influence. A parent who stays present while holding conviction retains the most important thing: access.

Words of Encouragement:

There will be seasons of parenting that feel like standing on shifting ground. Your child questions the faith you raised them in. Their sense of who they are seems unstable or borrowed from sources that alarm you. The culture speaks about sexuality and identity with a confidence and volume that your voice, however consistent, sometimes struggles to match. These are not small pressures. They are the defining interior battles of your child's developmental years, and the parent who is present for them is doing some of the most significant and least visible work of their entire life.

It is worth saying plainly: the questions your child is asking are not evidence that you have failed. A child who is wrestling with faith is a child who is taking it seriously enough to examine it. A child who is working out their identity is a child who has not simply accepted whatever the culture handed them. A child who brings difficult questions about sexuality to a parent, or who at least leaves the door open, is a child who still believes their parent is a safe place to bring hard things. None of that is failure. All of it is an invitation.

But it is also worth being honest about what this season costs a parent. Watching your child question the faith you have given your life to is painful in a way that is difficult to describe. It can feel like rejection. It can feel like loss. It can surface your own unresolved questions, the ones you set aside in the busyness of raising a family. And navigating a culture that speaks about identity and sexuality with complete confidence in a direction that contradicts Scripture requires a kind of sustained, calm conviction that is genuinely hard to maintain across years of pressure. You are allowed to find this hard. Finding it hard does not mean you are doing it wrong.

Scripture does not promise that faithfulness will be easy or that the results will be immediate. What it promises is presence. "Even though I walk through the darkest valley, I will fear no evil, for you are with me" (Psalm 23:4). God is in the valley with your child and with you. He is not watching from a distance, waiting to see how this resolves. He is actively at work in the questions, in the uncertainty, in the seasons that look from the outside like wandering but are, from His perspective, formation.

Think of the father in Luke 15 who watched his son walk away. He did not chase him down the road. He did not send messengers to bring him back by force. He waited, and he watched, and when his son was still a long way off, he saw him coming and ran. That father had no guarantee his son would return. He had only love that outlasted the distance. That is the posture this chapter is asking of you, not the posture of control, not the posture of panic, but the posture of a parent who keeps the light on and keeps watching the road.

Your child's faith, identity, and understanding of themselves are being formed across years, not settled in a single conversation. The investment you make today, speaking truth, staying present, refusing to let distance become the final word, is planting something that may not break the surface for a long time. But the God who formed your child before they were born (Jeremiah 1:5) has not lost sight of them in the questions. He who began a good work will carry it to completion (Philippians 1:6). That promise was not made conditionally. It was made by a God who keeps His word, in His time, in ways that are often only visible looking back.

So stay in the room. Keep speaking. Keep praying. Keep the relationship open even when the conversation is hard and the answers are not yet clear. "For I am sure that neither death nor life, nor angels nor rulers, nor things present nor things to come, nor powers, nor height nor depth, nor anything else in all creation, will be able to separate us from the love of God in Christ Jesus our Lord" (Romans 8:38-39). That love is holding your child in their most uncertain season. And it is holding you in yours.

10. Self-Harm: Understanding and Responding with Biblical Wisdom

Important Notice: *The guidance in this chapter is provided for educational and informational purposes only and does not constitute medical, psychological, or clinical advice. It is not a substitute for professional mental health care. If your child is experiencing self-harm behaviors, please consult a qualified mental health professional promptly. If your child is in immediate danger, call 988 (Suicide & Crisis Lifeline) or go to your nearest emergency room.*

Self-Harm Indicators appear in the Mental Health section of Warning Signs. The following detailed guidance expands on recognizing and responding to self-harm behaviors through a Christian perspective.

Understanding Self-Harm in Young People

> Self-harm (non-suicidal self-injury) typically functions as a coping mechanism for overwhelming emotional distress. While not usually intended as a suicide attempt, it can increase suicide risk over time if left unaddressed. As a parent, your compassionate, faith-informed response can help your child find healthier ways to process pain.

It is important for parents to understand the distinction between non-suicidal self-injury and suicidal behavior. Some young people who self-harm are not actively suicidal, while others may be at elevated suicide risk. Self-harm exists along a spectrum of risk, and suicidal intent must be carefully assessed rather than assumed or dismissed. Do not assume that because your child is self-harming they are planning to end their life, but do not assume the opposite either. Any self-harm should be taken seriously and carefully assessed by a qualified professional. If you are ever uncertain, err on the side of seeking professional evaluation.

> "*God is our refuge and strength, an ever-present help in trouble.*" (Psalm 46:1)

> **Important Note**: Research has found that self-harm behaviors can begin as early as age 10, and rates are increasing among pre-adolescent children. Parents of younger children need to be vigilant about these behaviors, as early intervention is crucial. The misconception that self-harm only affects teenagers may cause parents to miss warning signs in younger children. While the onset of self-harm commonly occurs during adolescence (12-14 years), children as young as 10 years old may begin engaging in these behaviors as they navigate complex emotions with limited coping skills and the inability to communicate effectively what they are feeling.

Understanding Self-Harm Patterns

While self-harm can affect anyone regardless of age or gender, parents should be aware that it typically occurs in areas of the body that are easily concealed by clothing, even during warm weather or athletic activities. This concealment is often deliberate. Children and teenagers who are engaging in self-harm are frequently skilled at hiding it, sometimes for months or years before a parent discovers it.

Behavioral patterns can vary by age and gender, and the methods used may differ as well. Some forms of self-harm are more visible than others, and some may be disguised as accidents, clumsiness, or the result of physical activity. A parent who notices repeated unexplained injuries, frequent use of bandages, or a consistent pattern of concealing certain areas of the body should take those observations seriously rather than accepting surface-level explanations.

If you suspect your child may be engaging in self-harm but are unsure what to look for or how to assess what you are seeing, consulting a licensed mental health professional is the appropriate next step. A trained clinician can conduct a proper assessment and provide guidance specific to your child's situation. The purpose of this chapter is to equip you to recognize the possibility and respond with compassion, not to provide a clinical assessment guide.

Warning Signs with Christ-Centered Response Examples

Physical Warning Signs

- **Unexplained cuts, burns, bruises, or scratches, particularly on arms, legs, or abdomen** *Response example:* "I noticed some marks on your arm when you reached for your glass. I'm concerned about you and wonder if you'd feel comfortable talking about what happened? I want you to know I'm here to listen without judgment."

- **Wearing concealing clothing (long sleeves, pants) regardless of weather or situation** *Response example:* "I've noticed you've been wearing long sleeves even during hot weather. I wonder if there's something making you uncomfortable or if there's anything you'd like to talk about? I care about what you're going through."

- **Avoiding activities that reveal skin (swimming, changing for gym)** *Response example:* "I noticed you've been sitting out during swim time lately, which is different from before. I'm wondering if something's changed or if there's something making you uncomfortable about participating? I'm here if you want to talk."

- **Frequent "accidents" that lack convincing explanations** *Response example:* "That's the third time this week you've mentioned getting hurt accidentally. I'm concerned that something else might be going on. Could we talk about what's happening? I want to understand and support you."

- **Finding sharp objects (razors, scissors, safety pins, pencil sharpener blades) or other items that could be used for harm in unusual places** *Response example:* "I found these items in your drawer when I was putting away laundry. I'm worried about what they might be used for. Could we have an honest conversation about this? I want to understand what you're going through."

- **Increased use of bandages, gauze, or antiseptic** *Response example:* "I've noticed you've been using a lot of bandages lately. I care about you and I'm concerned. Would you feel comfortable sharing with me what's been happening? I want to help however I can."

- **Fresh marks alongside older scars or healing wounds** *Response example:* "I can see that you have some wounds that look like they happened at different times. I'm really concerned about your wellbeing. Would you be willing to talk with me about what's going on? I want you to know that whatever you're dealing with, you don't have to face it alone."

Behavioral Warning Signs

- **Isolation from family and friends** *Response example:* "I've noticed you've been spending a lot more time by yourself lately. I miss our time together and I'm wondering if something's bothering you or if there's anything you'd like to talk about?"

- **Spending unusual amounts of time alone in bedroom or bathroom** *Response example:* "You've been spending a lot of time alone in your room lately. I respect your need for privacy, but I also want to make sure you're okay. Is there anything going on that I could help with, or would you like to talk?"

- **Expressing feelings of worthlessness, hopelessness, or self-loathing** *Response example:* "When you said you feel like you don't matter, it concerned me because you matter so much to me and to God. Would you be willing to share more about these feelings? I'd really like to understand what you're experiencing."

- **Interest in online content related to self-harm** *Response example:* "I noticed that your browser history showed searches about self-harm. This makes me worried about what you might be going through. Instead of jumping to conclusions, I'd like to understand what prompted those searches. Can we talk about it?"

- **Declining academic performance** *Response example:* "Your teacher mentioned that your grades have been dropping lately. I'm not upset about the grades themselves, but I wonder if something else is happening that might be making it hard to focus on school. Would you like to talk about what's been going on?"

- **Difficulty handling emotions or frequent emotional outbursts** *Response example:* "I've noticed that things seem to feel really intense for you lately, with some big emotional reactions. That makes me think you might be carrying some heavy feelings. I wonder if we could talk about what's happening inside that might be making things feel so overwhelming?"

- **Collecting or hoarding potential tools for self-harm** *Response example:* "I found these items in your room, and I'm concerned they might be used for hurting yourself. I want you to know that I'm not angry, but I am worried about you. Could we talk honestly about what's happening?"

- **Expressing that physical pain helps manage emotional pain** *Response example:* "When you mentioned that physical pain helps you feel better emotionally, it concerned me. That sounds like you're in a lot of emotional pain. I wonder if we could talk more about those difficult feelings and perhaps find healthier ways to address them together."

Faith-Integrated Response Guidance

When addressing self-harm with your child, consider these biblically-informed approaches:

A note on spiritual support: Prayer, Scripture, worship, and pastoral care can be deeply protective and stabilizing for a child who is struggling. These should absolutely be part of how a family responds to self-harm. However, spiritual support should complement, not replace, professional mental health care when self-harm or suicidality are present. Some parents, out of sincere faith, may be tempted to treat self-harm primarily as a spiritual problem to be resolved through spiritual means alone. This approach, while well-intentioned, can delay the professional intervention that protects your child's life. God works through skilled clinicians as readily as through prayer.

- **Start with compassion rather than shock or anger**
  "The Lord is compassionate and gracious, slow to anger, abounding in love." (Psalm 103:8)

- **Focus on the emotional pain behind the behavior**
  "The Lord is close to the brokenhearted and saves those who are crushed in spirit." (Psalm 34:18)

- **Emphasize God's love for their body as His temple**
  "Do you not know that your bodies are temples of the Holy Spirit, who is in you, whom you have received from God? You are not

your own; you were bought at a price. Therefore honor God with your bodies." (1 Corinthians 6:19-20)

- **Address shame with grace**
  "Therefore, there is now no condemnation for those who are in Christ Jesus." (Romans 8:1)

- **Pray together when appropriate**
  "Cast your cares on the LORD and he will sustain you; he will never let the righteous be shaken." (Psalm 55:22)

- **Seek professional help promptly**
  "Plans fail for lack of counsel, but with many advisers they succeed." (Proverbs 15:22)

Parents should not attempt to manage repetitive self-harm alone without professional evaluation and support. Whenever self-harm behavior is discovered, injuries are repetitive, self-harm escalates in severity, suicidality is unclear, emotional functioning is deteriorating, or trauma history is present, professional assessment is warranted. This is not a sign of parental failure. It is the responsible response of a parent who understands the limits of what love alone can address.

Biblical Intervention for Self-Harm

Remember that intervention requires balancing your spiritual guidance with appropriate professional help:

1. **Create a safe communication environment** where your child can speak honestly without fear of overreaction or judgment.

2. **Consult with Christian counselors** who specialize in adolescent mental health and self-harm. Many faith-based

counselors integrate biblical wisdom with effective therapeutic approaches.

3. **Remove potential self-harm implements** while discussing with your child why you're doing so, out of love, not punishment.

4. **Develop a safety plan** with your child and their mental health provider that includes:

   - Warning signs that indicate they need help
   - Healthy coping alternatives to try when urges arise
   - People they can contact when struggling
   - Emergency contacts and resources
   - Scripture verses or prayers that bring comfort

5. **Balance monitoring with trust-building**. While supervision is necessary, building trust is essential for long-term healing.

6. **Connect them with appropriate support groups**, either through your church or reputable Christian organizations that address teen mental health challenges.

7. **Remember that recovery is a process**, not an event. The journey toward healing often includes setbacks, but God's grace is sufficient even in our weakness (2 Corinthians 12:9).

A biblically-grounded approach recognizes that while self-harm is not God's design for managing pain, those who struggle with it are deeply loved by their Heavenly Father. Your Christ-centered response, combining grace and truth, compassion and action, reflects God's heart toward your hurting child.

Healthy Coping Alternatives to Self-Harm

"*Do not be anxious about anything, but in every situation, by prayer and petition, with thanksgiving, present your requests to God. And the peace of God, which transcends all understanding, will guard your hearts and your minds in Christ Jesus.*" (Philippians 4:6-7)

When young people turn to self-harm, they're often seeking relief from overwhelming emotions or trying to feel something when emotionally numb. These biblically grounded alternatives offer healthier ways to address these needs.

Grounding and Regulation Skills

In addition to the alternatives listed below, grounding and emotional regulation skills are among the most clinically effective tools for managing the urges that lead to self-harm. These skills work by helping the nervous system return to a regulated state when overwhelming emotion has triggered the urge to self-harm.

Body-based grounding exercises help a young person return to the present moment and out of the emotional overwhelm that precedes self-harm. Simple practices include slow, deliberate breathing, placing both feet flat on the floor and noticing the sensation of contact, holding something cold or textured, and naming five things that can be seen in the immediate environment. These are not distractions from the pain. They are physiological tools that interrupt the escalation cycle.

Emotional regulation skills help a young person identify and name what they are feeling before it reaches crisis level. Journaling, structured prayer, and honest conversation with a trusted adult are all effective regulation practices. A therapist trained in cognitive behavioral approaches or dialectical behavior therapy can provide your child with a personalized toolkit of regulation skills that go significantly beyond what any resource can offer.

Immediate Alternatives During Urges

These techniques can help in moments of intense distress when the urge to self-harm is strong:

- **The 5-4-3-2-1 Grounding Exercise**: Engage the five senses to anchor in the present moment:
  - 5 things you can see around you
  - 4 things you can touch or feel (like your Bible, a cross, or a smooth stone)
  - 3 things you can hear
  - 2 things you can smell (or like to smell)
  - 1 thing you can taste
  - Biblical connection: "*Be still, and know that I am God*" (Psalm 46:10)
- **Physical Redirection**:
  - Vigorous physical exercise (jumping jacks, running in place, brisk walking)
  - Rhythmic bilateral movement such as swimming, walking, or drumming, which engages the nervous system without physical harm
  - Controlled breathwork, slow, deliberate breathing to shift the body out of acute distress
  - Note: A Christian counselor or mental health professional can help identify the specific urge-management strategies that are most appropriate for your child's individual situation and stage of recovery.
  - Biblical connection: "*I discipline my body and keep it under control*" (1 Corinthians 9:27)
- **Emotional Release**:
  - Tear or crumple paper
  - Scream into or punch a pillow

    - Squeeze stress balls
    - Create intense art expressing feelings
    - Biblical connection: "*My tears have been my food day and night*" (Psalm 42:3) – David openly expressed his emotions
- **Delaying Technique**: Commit to waiting 15 minutes before acting on the urge, using that time to pray, read Scripture, or call a support person.
    - Biblical connection: "*But they who wait for the LORD shall renew their strength*" (Isaiah 40:31)

Faith-Based Emotional Regulation Skills

These practices help develop longer-term emotional management:

- **Biblical Meditation**: Focus on a short Scripture passage or even a single verse:
    - "*Finally, brothers and sisters, whatever is true, whatever is noble, whatever is right, whatever is pure, whatever is lovely, whatever is admirable, if anything is excellent or praiseworthy, think about such things.*" (Philippians 4:8)
    - Write the verse on an index card to carry at all times
    - Set it as a phone wallpaper for frequent viewing
- **Breath Prayer**: Combine breathing exercises with short Scripture phrases:
    - Inhale: "The Lord is my shepherd"
    - Exhale: "I shall not want"
    - Or simply repeating "Jesus" or "Abba Father" with each breath

  - Biblical connection: God breathed life into humans (Genesis 2:7), and the word for Spirit (ruach) also means breath

- **Lament Journaling**: Writing honest prayers of pain and confusion:

  - Based on the biblical practice of lament seen throughout Psalms

  - Follows the pattern: Address God → Express pain → Remember God's faithfulness → Choose to trust

  - Biblical connection: "*How long, O LORD? Will you forget me forever?*" (Psalm 13:1)

- **Christian Mindfulness**: Focused attention on God's presence in the present moment:

  - Notice where you are and that God is present with you

  - Pay attention to your body as God's temple

  - Observe thoughts without judgment, surrendering them to God

  - Biblical connection: "*Be transformed by the renewal of your mind*" (Romans 12:2)

Developing Healthy Emotional Practices

Help your child build these regular habits for emotional and spiritual health:

- **Creative Expression**:
  - Art therapy (drawing, painting, sculpting) to express emotions
  - Music (playing instruments, singing, or listening to worship music)
  - Writing poetry, stories, or song lyrics
  - Biblical connection: David's psalms expressed the full range of human emotions
- **Physical Self-Care**:
  - Regular exercise as stewardship of God's temple
  - Balanced nutrition and adequate sleep
  - Time in nature appreciating God's creation
  - Biblical connection: "*Or do you not know that your body is a temple of the Holy Spirit within you?*" (1 Corinthians 6:19)
- **Spiritual Disciplines**:
  - Regular Bible study and Scripture memorization
  - Structured prayer times
  - Worship through music or movement
  - Biblical connection: "*They devoted themselves to the apostles' teaching and to fellowship, to the breaking of bread and to prayer*" (Acts 2:42)

- **Relational Support**:
    - Authentic youth group participation
    - Mentoring relationships with trusted adult believers
    - Service to others (volunteering shifts focus outward)
    - Biblical connection: "*Bear one another's burdens, and so fulfill the law of Christ*" (Galatians 6:2)

Age-Appropriate Considerations

When introducing these alternatives, consider developmental stages:

- **Ages 10-13**: More concrete techniques work best (physical activities, simple breathing exercises, art)
- **Ages 14-17**: Can engage with more abstract practices (meditation, visualization, deeper journaling)
- **Ages 18-24**: Capable of more sophisticated spiritual disciplines and self-directed practices

Creating a "Spiritual First Aid Kit"

Work with your child to create a physical kit containing items that engage multiple senses and connect to their faith:

- **Visual**: Scripture cards, encouraging photos, Christian symbols
- **Tactile**: Cross to hold, prayer beads, smooth stones with Bible verses
- **Auditory**: Playlist of worship songs, recorded prayers or Scriptures
- **Olfactory**: Scented items that promote calm (lavender, etc.)

- **Gustatory**: Mints or other strong flavors to redirect attention

This kit should be readily accessible during difficult emotional moments.

"*For God has not given us a spirit of fear, but of power and of love and of a sound mind.*" (2 Timothy 1:7 (NKJV))

Remember that implementing these alternatives works best when part of comprehensive care that includes professional support. These practices complement, not replace, appropriate counseling and medical treatment when needed. Through your guidance and God's grace, your child can discover healthier ways to process pain while growing closer to their Heavenly Father who deeply loves them.

When to Seek Crisis Intervention

Immediate professional help is needed if:

- **Self-harm Becomes Severe:** Wounds requiring medical attention
- **Suicidal Thoughts Emerge:** Any mention of wanting to die requires immediate response
- **Escalating Patterns:** Increasing frequency or severity of self-harm
- **Failed Safety Plans:** Inability to maintain safety despite interventions
- **Significant Functional Impact:** Inability to maintain basic activities of daily living

In emergency situations, call 988 (National Suicide Prevention Lifeline), go to your local emergency room, or call 911.

Words of Encouragement:

"But they who wait for the LORD shall renew their strength; they shall mount up with wings like eagles; they shall run and not be weary; they shall walk and not faint." (Isaiah 40:31)

Parenting a child who struggles with self-harm can feel like an overwhelming journey, sometimes leaving you feeling isolated. In these difficult moments, remember that you are never alone in this valley. The Good Shepherd, who leaves the ninety-nine to find the one, is walking alongside both you and your child right now.

When you first discovered your child's self-harm, your heart may have shattered in ways you never imagined possible. That heartbreak mirrors God's own heart for your child, a love so profound that it feels every wound. Your tears are precious to the Lord, who lovingly keeps them in His bottle (Psalm 56:8).

There will be days when progress seems elusive, when you question every decision, and when your prayers feel like they're hitting a ceiling. In those challenging times, remember that faith is not the absence of doubt but the choice to reach out to God even when the path ahead isn't clear. Just like the father who cried out, "Lord, I believe; help my unbelief!" (Mark 9:24), you too will find grace in your honest struggle.

The enemy may try to convince you that you've failed as a parent, that if only you had done something differently, prayed more fervently, or recognized the signs sooner, your child wouldn't be in pain. But that voice is not from your loving Father. God does not condemn you; instead, He stands ready to equip you for this battle: "For God gave us a spirit not of fear but of power and love and self-discipline" (2 Timothy 1:7).

Your consistent presence, even when imperfect, speaks volumes to your child. Like the persistent widow in Luke 18, your unwavering advocacy, both before earthly helpers and at the throne of heaven, makes a difference that may not be visible today but will bear fruit in time. "Let us not become weary in doing good, for at the proper time we will reap a harvest if we do not give up" (Galatians 6:9).

Keep in mind that healing often doesn't follow a straight path. Setbacks may occur alongside progress, much like Israel's journey to the Promised Land, filled with wilderness wanderings. Yet, each small victory matters, every day without self-harm, every honest conversation, and every time your child chooses a healthy coping skill over a harmful one.

Throughout Scripture, God demonstrates His ability to bring good out of pain, not causing it, but transforming what was meant for harm into something beautiful. Joseph's powerful words to his brothers echo through time: "You intended to harm me, but God intended it for good" (Genesis 50:20). This painful chapter can become part of a powerful testimony of God's faithfulness and healing in your family's story.

Take heart, faithful parent. Your labor of love is not in vain. The God who counts every hair on your child's head (Luke 12:7) sees your sacrificial care. The same power that raised Christ from the dead is at work in you and your child (Ephesians 1:19-20). Whatever lies ahead, you can trust that "neither death nor life, neither angels nor demons, neither the present nor the future, nor any powers, neither height nor depth, nor anything else in all creation, will be able to separate us from the love of God that is in Christ Jesus our Lord" (Romans 8:38-39).

Hold fast to hope. Your child's story is still being written, and the Author of Life specializes in crafting beautiful redemption stories.

11. Suicide Intervention: A Life-Saving Guide for Parents

A Steadfast Critical Response Resource

Important Notice: *The guidance in this chapter is provided for educational and informational purposes only and does not constitute medical, psychological, or clinical advice. It is not a substitute for professional mental health care. If your child has expressed suicidal thoughts or you believe they are at risk, please contact a qualified mental health professional immediately. If your child is in immediate danger, call 988 (Suicide & Crisis Lifeline) or go to your nearest emergency room.*

Understanding the Scope: Current Statistics

Suicide remains a significant public health concern among young people today:

- Suicide is the second leading cause of death for teens and young adults ages 10–34, making it one of the most urgent preventable causes of premature death in the United States. (The Jed Foundation, 2024)
- According to the American Foundation for Suicide Prevention (AFSP), suicide rates among 15– to 24-year-olds decreased 10% between 2021 and 2022, from 15.2 to 13.6 per 100,000. While this is encouraging, experts note that actual rates may be higher than recorded figures due to well-documented underreporting, some deaths are classified as accidental or undetermined for a variety of reasons. (AFSP, 2024)
- Suicidal thoughts are far more widespread than completed suicides. The Substance Abuse and Mental Health Services Administration (SAMHSA) reports that 12.3% of adolescents aged 12–17 had serious thoughts of suicide in the past year, and 3.3% made an attempt. Many young people who die by

suicide gave some warning to those around them beforehand. (SAMHSA National Survey on Drug Use and Health, 2024)
- Among high school students nationwide, approximately 20% reported seriously considering suicide in the past year, and nearly 1 in 10 reported making an attempt. Girls are more likely to attempt suicide, while boys are four times more likely to die by suicide, primarily due to the use of more lethal means. (Johns Hopkins Medicine; The Jed Foundation, 2024)
- The National Institute of Mental Health (NIMH) reports that among young adults aged 18–25, 12.6% experienced serious suicidal thoughts in the past year, the highest prevalence of any adult age group. Suicide risk is shaped by a range of individual, relational, and community factors, reinforcing the importance of early, relationship-based prevention. (NIMH, 2024)

It is also important for parents to understand that suicidality rarely exists in isolation. It is most commonly accompanied by other medical or psychiatric conditions that require their own treatment. The most frequent contributors include depression, trauma disorders, bipolar disorder, substance use, psychosis, neurodevelopmental differences, severe anxiety, chronic shame, and prolonged social isolation. This does not mean that every child who struggles with these conditions is at risk for suicide. It means that when suicidal thinking is present, a thorough evaluation for underlying conditions is an essential part of the response. Treating the suicidality without addressing the underlying contributors is like treating a symptom without treating the cause.

Recognizing Warning Signs

As a parent, being vigilant about warning signs is an act of love and care. Warning signs may include:

Verbal Indicators

- Direct statements: "I want to die" or "I'm going to kill myself"
- Indirect statements: "I wish I could fall asleep and never wake up again"
- Talking about being a burden: "Everyone would be better off without me"
- Expressing hopelessness: "Things will never get better"
- Expressing unbearable pain: "I can't take it anymore"

Behavioral Changes

- Making final arrangements (e.g., making funeral arrangements, writing a will, giving away prized possessions)
- Preoccupation with death
- Withdrawing from friends, family, and activities once enjoyed
- Increased substance use
- Engaging in risky or self-destructive behavior
- Researching methods of suicide online
- Expressing hopelessness, being isolated, sleeping too little or too much and increased substance use

Emotional and Physical Signs

- Persistent sadness, emptiness, or emotional numbness
- Irritability or increased agitation
- Extreme mood swings
- Changes in eating or sleeping patterns
- Overwhelming shame or guilt
- Physical health complaints possibly linked to emotional distress
- Lack of interest in appearance

Digital Warning Signs

- Posts about death, hopelessness, or wanting to disappear
- Dramatic changes in online activity (either significantly increased or decreased)
- Increased access to social media and negative online media
- Sharing goodbye messages or resolving conflicts suddenly
- Increased consumption of content related to suicide or self-harm

Biblical Perspective on Suicide Intervention

While the Bible doesn't directly address suicide prevention as we understand it today, Scripture provides powerful principles for intervention:

- **The Value of Each Life**: "*Are not five sparrows sold for two pennies? Yet not one of them is forgotten by God. Indeed, the very hairs of your head are all numbered. Don't be afraid; you are worth more than many sparrows.*" (Luke 12:6-7)

- **Bearing Burdens**: "*Carry each other's burdens, and in this way you will fulfill the law of Christ.*" (Galatians 6:2)

- **Community Support**: "*Two are better than one... If either of them falls down, one can help the other up.*" (Ecclesiastes 4:9-10)

- **Hope in Darkness**: "*Do not gloat over me, my enemy! Though I have fallen, I will rise. Though I sit in darkness, the Lord will be my light.*" (Micah 7:8)

A pastoral note for families of deep faith: Parents who hold strong theological convictions sometimes inadvertently interpret suicidal thoughts or behaviors through a spiritual or moral lens alone. In some religious contexts, suicidality can be viewed as spiritual weakness, demonic oppression, a lack of faith in God's goodness, or even moral rebellion. These interpretations, however sincerely held, can intensify shame, increase secrecy, and delay the professional intervention that could save your child's life. A child who fears that their suicidal thoughts will be treated as evidence of spiritual failure is far less likely to disclose them honestly.

Suicidal suffering should never be reduced to spiritual failure, weakness, rebellion, or lack of faith. It is complex, and it almost always involves psychological, relational, developmental, neurobiological, and trauma-related factors alongside any spiritual dimensions. Spiritual care, prayer, Scripture, and Christian community can be deeply stabilizing and should absolutely be part of your response. They should complement professional care, not substitute for it.

The Seekers ALS Approach: Alert, Listen, Serve

The Seekers International Foundation's (iseekers.org) ALS Approach was developed in alignment with established, evidence-based suicide intervention principles and frameworks, and integrates those foundations with a Biblical understanding of human dignity, community, and redemptive hope. Its three steps, Alert, Listen, Serve, reflect the core elements recognized across professional intervention models: compassionate engagement, active listening, and movement toward safety and support.

ALERT: Engage with Compassion

1. Create a Safe Place
    - Choose a private, comfortable environment
    - Minimize distractions (put away phones)
    - Maintain a calm, non-judgmental demeanor
    - Begin with care and concern, not accusation or panic
2. Remove Barriers to Connection
    - Set aside labels and stereotypes that might hinder genuine communication
    - Recognize that the person may be caught in what feels like a "riptide of despair" ™
    - Commit to being fully present with 100% of your attention

LISTEN: Practice Active Listening

1. Effective Listening Techniques
    - Give full attention through eye contact and responsive body language
    - Allow silences without rushing to fill them
    - Validate feelings without minimizing them
    - Avoid dismissive statements like "You have nothing to be sad about"

- Listen for underlying pain rather than focusing only on actions
- Reflect back what you hear: "It sounds like you're feeling..."

2. Use Body Language Effectively
   - Nod occasionally to show understanding
   - Use facial expressions that show concern and care
   - Keep your posture open and inviting
   - Encourage continued sharing with affirming small verbal comments
3. Ask Your Child Directly About Suicide
   - Start with observations: "I've noticed you've been [specific behavior]. I'm concerned about you."
   - Follow with direct questions using clear language:
     - "Are you having thoughts about killing yourself?"
     - "Are you thinking about suicide?"
     - "Do you sometimes wish you weren't alive anymore?"
   - Remain calm regardless of your child's answer
   - Affirm that you're asking because you love and care deeply about your child

4. Listen to Your Child's Reasons

    - Allow your child to express fully why they are considering suicide
    - Resist the urge to offer quick solutions or judgments
    - Practice using silence as a powerful tool for encouraging deeper sharing
    - Understand that your child needs to know you've truly heard and understood their pain

SERVE: Move Toward Safety

1. Assess Immediate Risk

    - Ask your child about specific plans, timing, means, and access
    - Higher specificity generally indicates higher risk

    There are circumstances that require immediate emergency intervention rather than at-home management. If your child has a specific suicide plan, has expressed clear intent, has access to means, cannot commit to immediate safety, is showing signs of psychosis or intoxication, has a history of prior attempts, is severely agitated, or is expressing a rapidly escalating sense of hopelessness, do not wait. Call 988 or take your child to the nearest emergency room immediately. These are not situations where parental presence and conversation are sufficient. They are situations where professional emergency evaluation is required. Seeking emergency care in these moments is not an overreaction. It is the most loving thing a parent can do.

- o Determine if your child has immediate access to lethal means
- o Calmly move through the space with your child and remove access to any potential means of harm. Do not leave your child alone during this time.

2. Ensure Immediate Safety

- o Remove your child's access to potential means of harm
- o Secure medications, including over-the-counter drugs, away from your child
- o Any guns in your home should be unloaded, locked, and kept out of your child's reach
- o Do not leave your child alone if they are at imminent risk

3. Create a Survival Map

- o Work collaboratively: Work alongside your child to identify their own reasons for living, their support network, and the coping strategies that feel most accessible to them
- o Identify dangers: Discuss issues with substances, previous attempts, mental health history
- o Re-establish life anchors: Identify family members, friends, clergy, or counselors your child can call
- o Look for "life anchors" - reasons for living that are still important to your child
- o Help your child move from focusing on death to focusing on life

4. Get Professional Help

    - o For immediate danger, call 988 (Suicide & Crisis Lifeline) or take your child to the emergency room
    - o Contact your child's doctor or mental health provider
    - o If your child has a therapist, contact them for guidance
    - o Never agree to keep your child's suicidal thoughts a secret

Throughout this chapter, the guidance is designed to help you engage your child with compassion, presence, and clarity during a crisis. Parental love and attunement are profoundly protective. However, parental support should not replace professional suicide assessment and intervention. A parent who responds beautifully in a crisis moment but then manages the situation alone, without professional evaluation, is carrying a weight that no parent is equipped to carry alone. Suicidal crises frequently require formal risk assessment, psychiatric evaluation, trauma assessment, medication evaluation, and higher levels of care. Seeking that help is not a failure of faith or of parenting. It is wisdom.

Long-Term Support and Recovery

After the immediate crisis, focus on building a support system:

Professional Support

- Connect with mental health professionals experienced in youth suicide prevention
- Consider faith-integrated therapy that respects your Christian values
- Follow through with recommended treatment plans

- Attend family therapy sessions when recommended

Home Support

- Create a safety plan together with professional guidance
- Maintain open communication about feelings
- Balance supervision with appropriate space
- Empathize and listen. Don't minimize their feelings, it can affect how they reach out for support in the future
- Encourage your child to develop healthy coping mechanisms (exercise, creative expression, spiritual practices)
- Consistently emphasize hope and God's presence in suffering to your child

Spiritual Support

- Pray with and for your child (while avoiding spiritualizing mental health issues)
- Connect with supportive faith community members
- Share scripture that emphasizes God's love, not condemnation
- Explore appropriate spiritual disciplines that might bring comfort
- Consult with pastors or Christian counselors who understand both faith and mental health

Supporting Siblings and Family

Suicide concerns affect the entire family:

- Provide age-appropriate information to siblings

- Allow siblings to express their fears and concerns
- Consider family therapy to strengthen communication
- Take care of your own mental health needs as parents
- Reach out to support groups for parents in similar situations

A Note on Contagion Risk

Research on suicide contagion, sometimes called the "clustering effect", has established that exposure to a suicide attempt or death by suicide within a family or peer group can increase risk for others, particularly young people. This does not mean the topic should be avoided; open, compassionate conversation is protective. What it does mean is that how the subject is discussed matters. When talking with siblings or other family members about a loved one's suicidal crisis, focus on the pain the person was experiencing and the support they are now receiving, rather than on the specific means or circumstances involved. Avoid language that romanticizes or dramatizes the crisis. Model honest, grounded, hope-filled communication, and encourage siblings to come to you with any of their own fears or struggles. If you have concerns about another child in the household following a sibling's crisis, do not wait, contact a mental health professional promptly.

Prevention for the Future

Whether your child has experienced suicidal thoughts or you want to build protective factors:

- Foster genuine connection daily
- Help them build healthy peer relationships
- Encourage involvement in faith community and service
- Teach and model healthy ways to manage emotions

- Leading suicide prevention organizations including AFSP and SAMHSA stress the importance of a comprehensive, relationship-centered approach to prevention that begins long before a crisis occurs, and includes support for those at increased risk.

- Build resilience through faith practices and life skills

Life Protectors and Promoters

Help your child identify resources that strengthen their will to live:

- **Thoughts** that encourage them and help them remember what matters
- **Behaviors** they want to do more often or that remind them of their value
- **Beliefs** they live by and that bring them hope
- **Decisions** they need to make or avoid for their wellbeing
- **Things** they treasure or that bring them pleasure
- **Times** when they know they need a break or assistance
- **People** they admire, who need them, or whose lives they want to follow

Follow Up

The follow-up is your responsibility:

- Make sure your child receives the help you arranged
- Continue checking in with your child consistently and regularly
- Be persistent in maintaining connection with your child
- Communicate your ongoing love, care and concern to your child

Life Anchors and Faith Foundation

Having strong life anchors, relationships, purpose, and hope, is essential for mental wellbeing. As parents, you can help your child identify and strengthen these critical connections to life:

- **Relationship Anchors**: Foster your child's sense of belonging within family, faith community, and healthy friendships. Remind them they are deeply loved by you and by God. "*For I am convinced that neither death nor life... will be able to separate us from the love of God that is in Christ Jesus our Lord*" (Romans 8:38-39).

- **Purpose Anchors**: Help your child discover how their unique gifts can serve others and fulfill God's calling. "*For we are God's handiwork, created in Christ Jesus to do good works, which God prepared in advance for us to do*" (Ephesians 2:10).

- **Hope Anchors**: Nurture a biblical perspective that sees beyond present circumstances to God's promises. "*For I know the plans I have for you," declares the LORD, "plans to prosper you and not to harm you, plans to give you hope and a future*" (Jeremiah 29:11).

- **Identity Anchors**: Continuously affirm your child's worth as created in God's image and deeply valued. "*Are not five sparrows sold for two pennies? Yet not one of them is forgotten by God... You are worth more than many sparrows*" (Luke 12:6-7).

- **Faith Anchors**: Help your child develop spiritual practices that sustain them in difficult times, prayer, Scripture, worship, and Christian community. "*They devoted themselves to the apostles' teaching and to fellowship, to the breaking of bread and to prayer*" (Acts 2:42).

Ultimately, Jesus Christ is our most secure anchor, as Scripture tells us: "*We have this hope as an anchor for the soul, firm and secure*" (Hebrews 6:19). While your child may need professional mental health support during crisis times, the development of these life anchors provides enduring resilience.

When teaching your child about these anchors, remember to:

- Make the connections explicit, help them name their anchors
- Celebrate even small expressions of connection to these anchors
- Model how you yourself rely on these anchors in your own life
- Be patient, anchor development strengthens over time and require trust
- Provide opportunities to test and experience these anchors in daily life

When other supports may shift, Christ remains the unchanging rock upon which your child can build their life. "*The name of the Lord is a fortified tower; the righteous run to it and are safe*" (Proverbs 18:10).

SEEKERS SUICIDE INTERVENTION CORPS TRAINING

For parents who want to deepen their understanding and ability to respond to suicide risks, the Seekers International Foundation offers specialized training through the Suicide Intervention Corps. This training equips parents, youth workers, and other caring adults with evidence-based tools for intervention and prevention. Learn more and register for training at https://ssic.iseekers.org.

Remember that seeking help for suicidal thoughts is an act of courage and faith, not weakness. As Christians, we believe in a God who walks with us through the valley of the shadow of death (Psalm 23:4) and who brings hope even in the darkest circumstances.

After the Crisis: What the Days and Weeks Ahead Require

Research consistently shows that suicide risk does not disappear once a crisis moment passes. In fact, risk can increase in the days and weeks immediately following disclosure or hospitalization, as the child returns to the stressors that contributed to the crisis while still in a fragile state. The period immediately after a crisis requires intentional, sustained attention.

Concrete steps for the post-crisis period include: following through with all recommended therapy appointments without gaps, coordinating with your child's school to ensure appropriate support and reduced pressure during recovery, monitoring sleep patterns which are both a risk factor and an indicator of recovery, supporting medication compliance if medication has been prescribed, maintaining honest and open family communication without treating the subject as off-limits, restricting access to lethal means on an ongoing basis rather than just during the acute crisis, and staying in close contact with your child's mental health provider about any signs of regression.

Your child does not need you to pretend the crisis did not happen. They need you to stay close, stay engaged, and stay connected to the professional support system that is helping them find their way back.

Words of Encouragement:

"For I am convinced that neither death nor life, neither angels nor demons, neither the present nor the future, nor any powers, neither height nor depth, nor anything else in all creation, will be able to separate us from the love of God that is in Christ Jesus our Lord." (Romans 8:38-39)

Confronting suicide concerns takes incredible courage, and your willingness to tackle this difficult topic head-on may literally save your child's life. By seeking information and taking action, you're already demonstrating a deep and attentive love that truly makes a difference.

Remember, Scripture reassures us that "The LORD is close to the brokenhearted and saves those who are crushed in spirit" (Psalm 34:18). This promise stands strong, even in our darkest moments. Each person experiences pain, both physical and mental, differently. The waves of difficulty that crash into our lives can affect individuals in unique ways. For some, challenges may feel like a minor current to navigate; for others, the same circumstances can feel like a devastating tsunami that uproots everything. As Solomon wisely noted, "Each heart knows its own bitterness, and no one else can share its joy" (Proverbs 14:10).

Never underestimate the profound influence you have as a parent. God has specifically placed you in your child's life for a divine purpose. When Moses instructed the Israelites about teaching God's commands, he emphasized the everyday impact parents have: "Impress them on your children. Talk about them when you sit at home and when you walk along the road, when you lie down and when you get up" (Deuteronomy 6:7). Your consistent presence, sitting together, walking alongside them, being there at the start and end of each day, creates a secure foundation, even amid struggles.

Your words carry incredible weight. Proverbs reminds us that "The tongue has the power of life and death" (Proverbs 18:21), and this truth resonates deeply for parents. Your affirmations about your child's value, purpose, and future can stand strong against the destructive lies that fuel suicidal thoughts. When you speak words of hope into seemingly hopeless situations, you're participating in God's redemptive work.

Your actions demonstrate God's unfailing love. The Bible shows us that God's love is not just spoken but actively demonstrated through action, "This is how we know what love is: Jesus Christ laid down his life for us" (1 John 3:16). When you persist in seeking help for your child, make yourself available in the middle of the night, and learn new skills to support their recovery, you're providing tangible evidence of their immense worth. This living message can penetrate even the deepest despair.

Even in the valley of the shadow of death, God promises to be with us (Psalm 23:4). He can use you as His hands and feet, providing comfort and guidance. Your parental influence isn't confined to childhood; it shapes your son or daughter throughout their lives. As you walk this challenging path, hold fast to the truth that "God has not given us a spirit of fear, but of power and of love and of a sound mind" (2 Timothy 1:7, NKJV). Your presence, persistence, and prayer matter immensely on this journey. You are not alone in this struggle, and neither is your child.

Remember, God Himself models perfect parenting. He pursues us when we stray, comforts us in our pain, sets loving boundaries, speaks truth, extends grace, and never abandons us, regardless of our choices. "Though my father and mother forsake me, the LORD will receive me" (Psalm 27:10). Your imperfect yet genuine efforts to reflect these qualities make a difference that goes far beyond what you can currently see. Even when progress seems slow or nonexistent, trust that "the God of all grace, who called you to his eternal glory in Christ, after you have suffered a little while, will himself restore you and make you strong, firm and steadfast" (1 Peter 5:10).

12. Nurturing Your Relationship Through Challenges

"There is no fear in love. But perfect love drives out fear, because fear has to do with punishment. The one who fears is not made perfect in love. We love because he first loved us." (1 John 4:18-19)

Building Trust and Connection Across Developmental Stages

The foundation of helping your child through any crisis is a relationship of trust and connection. This foundation must be adapted as your child grows through different developmental stages::

Ages 10-13

- **Quality Time**: Schedule regular one-on-one activities your child enjoys. "*These commandments that I give you today are to be on your hearts. Impress them on your children. Talk about them when you sit at home and when you walk along the road, when you lie down and when you get up*" (Deuteronomy 6:6-7).
- **Physical Affection**: Offer appropriate touch based on your child's comfort level, recognizing that Jesus welcomed children into His arms (Mark 10:13-16).
- **Affirming Words**: Provide specific praise for character, not just achievement. "*Therefore encourage one another and build each other up, just as in fact you are doing*" (1 Thessalonians 5:11).

- **Consistency**: Be reliable and present, creating security through your dependable presence, as God is described as *"the same yesterday and today and forever"* (Hebrews 13:8).

- **Playfulness**: Maintain humor and fun in your relationship, for *"a cheerful heart is good medicine"* (Proverbs 17:22).

Ages 14-17

- **Respect Growing Independence**: Acknowledge their emerging adult identity while providing guidance. *"Train up a child in the way he should go; even when he is old he will not depart from it"* (Proverbs 22:6).

- **Listen More Than Lecture**: Create space for their perspectives, remembering to be *"quick to listen, slow to speak"* (James 1:19).

- **Shared Activities**: Find new common interests as they mature, investing in relationship as Jesus did with His disciples.

- **Apologize When Needed**: Model humility and repentance when you make mistakes. *"Therefore confess your sins to each other and pray for each other so that you may be healed"* (James 5:16).

- **Celebrate Their Unique Identity**: Affirm who they're becoming as made in God's image with specific calling and gifts. *"For you created my inmost being; you knit me together in my mother's womb... I am fearfully and wonderfully made"* (Psalm 139:13-14).

Ages 18-24

- **Adult-to-Adult Communication**: Transition to more peer-like interaction that honors their maturity. "*When I was a child, I talked like a child, I thought like a child, I reasoned like a child. When I became a man, I put the ways of childhood behind me*" (1 Corinthians 13:11).

- **Redefine Traditions**: Evolve family practices for their changing life stage, creating new ways to connect that respect their autonomy.

- **Appropriate Distance**: Respect boundaries while maintaining connection, offering guidance when invited. "*A person's wisdom yields patience; it is to one's glory to overlook an offense*" (Proverbs 19:11).

- **Shared Faith Conversations**: Engage in deeper spiritual discussions as fellow believers, discussing matters of faith as Paul did with Timothy.

- **Life Coaching**: Offer wisdom while honoring their decision-making. "*Listen to advice and accept discipline, and at the end you will be counted among the wise*" (Proverbs 19:20).

✈ FROM THE FIELD

We have had our share of struggles, tragedies, disappointments, and failures as a family. I will not pretend otherwise. But I can say honestly that after all of it (the international years, the repatriation, the things we missed and the things we carried) we are closer now than we have ever been.

My children are older now, the youngest having just turned eighteen. And I find that the role I am called to as their father is shifting in a way I did not entirely anticipate but have come to embrace. We are transitioning from stern parents to gentle advisors and cheerleaders. When your children reach the age of full responsibility for their own lives, you have to step back and let them drive. That is not abdication; it is trust. Trust that God is actively working in them. Trust that what you poured into them over the years took root, even when you couldn't see it.

I speak with my children every day. I pray for them every morning and every night. Not because I am anxious about them, but because they are the most important people in my life and I want God to know that I know it. Sometimes the most powerful intervention a parent can make is simply to stay present, stay praying, and stay cheering.

Supporting Without Enabling

One of the greatest challenges parents face is helping their child through difficulties without removing the growth opportunities those challenges provide:

- **Distinguish Struggles from Crises**: Different situations require different responses. Struggles are opportunities for growth; crises require intervention. "*There is a time for everything, and a season for every activity under the heavens*" (Ecclesiastes 3:1).

- **Offer Wisdom, Not Control**: Share insights without making decisions for your child. "*I will instruct you and teach you in the way you should go; I will counsel you with my loving eye on you*" (Psalm 32:8).

- **Resource Provision**: Provide tools and support, not solutions. Equip your child to face challenges rather than removing them, as God provides what we need but still calls us to "*put on the full armor of God*" (Ephesians 6:11).

- **Respect Agency**: Honor your child's freedom to choose, even when you disagree. God similarly gives us choice while guiding us toward His best. "*I have set before you life and death, blessing and curse. Therefore choose life*" (Deuteronomy 30:19, ESV).

- **Natural Consequences**: Allow your child to experience appropriate results of choices when safe. "*Do not be deceived: God cannot be mocked. A man reaps what he sows*" (Galatians 6:7).

Self-Care for Christian Parents

Your ability to support your child effectively depends significantly on your own spiritual and emotional health:

- **Prayer Priority**: Maintain consistent intercession and surrender concerning your child. "*Do not be anxious about anything, but in every situation, by prayer and petition, with thanksgiving, present your requests to God*" (Philippians 4:6).

- **Christian Community Support**: Connect with other parents for encouragement and wisdom sharing. "*And let us consider how we may spur one another on toward love and good deeds, not giving up meeting together, as some are in the habit of doing, but encouraging one another*" (Hebrews 10:24-25).

- **Marriage Nurture**: If married, strengthen your partnership during parenting challenges, remembering that "*a cord of three strands is not quickly broken*" (Ecclesiastes 4:12).

- **Personal Growth**: Continue your own spiritual development, for you cannot give what you do not possess. "*But grow in the grace and knowledge of our Lord and Savior Jesus Christ*" (2 Peter 3:18).

- **Healthy Boundaries**: Know your limitations and respect your needs, following Jesus' example of withdrawing to pray and rest (Luke 5:16).

Moving Forward After Crisis

When your child has experienced suicidal thoughts or other significant mental health challenges, rebuilding your relationship may require intentional effort:

- **Rebuild Trust Gradually**: If trust was broken through the crisis period, restore it through consistent small acts of reliability and honesty.

- **Create New Patterns**: Establish healthy new routines that support ongoing mental wellness for the entire family.

- **Celebrate Progress**: Acknowledge even small steps forward in your child's healing journey. "*Let us not become weary in doing good, for at the proper time we will reap a harvest if we do not give up*" (Galatians 6:9).

- **Process Your Own Emotions**: Work through your own feelings of fear, guilt, or grief with trusted support people or professional help.

- **Prepare for Setbacks**: Develop a calm, prepared response for potential recurrences of concerning symptoms or behavior.

You Were Made for Community

This book was written to give you language for what you are seeing, tools for how to respond, and a biblical foundation for the hardest moments of parenting. But a book, no matter how thorough, cannot do what community can. It cannot sit with you in the middle of the night when you are afraid. It cannot tell you that someone else has been exactly where you are and found a way through. It cannot offer the irreplaceable gift of being known by people who understand from the inside.

WayFinder™ was built for that purpose.

WayFinder™ is a community and training platform for internationally mobile families, missionary parents, and everyone navigating the challenges of raising children in a world that moves faster and cuts deeper than any previous generation has faced. It is a place where the families this book was written for can find one another, grow together, and be equipped to thrive rather than simply survive.

If this book has given you something you needed, WayFinder™ is where the journey continues.

You can learn more and join us at: steadfastltd.io

Scan to join WayFinder™

Navigate Change. Thrive Together.

Words of Encouragement

"But those who hope in the LORD will renew their strength. They will soar on wings like eagles; they will run and not grow weary, they will walk and not be faint." (Isaiah 40:31)

Walking alongside a child through mental health struggles can be one of the most challenging journeys you'll ever embark on. There will be moments when the weight feels unbearable, and you might question whether your efforts truly make a difference. In those dark valleys, remember: you are never alone. The God who formed your child in the womb is right there with you, walking through every shadow.

Scripture reassures us that "The LORD is close to the brokenhearted and saves those who are crushed in spirit" (Psalm 34:18). This promise extends not only to your child in their suffering but also to you in your moments of parental anguish. The same Lord who counts the hairs on your child's head (Luke 12:7) sees every tear you shed, every sleepless night you endure, and every desperate prayer whispered in the stillness.

There will be days when you feel inadequate for the task ahead. But let those feelings remind you of the truth: "My grace is sufficient for you, for my power is made perfect in weakness" (2 Corinthians 12:9). Your willingness to keep showing up, reaching out, and loving through the darkness speaks volumes to your child. It reflects the heart of your Heavenly Father, who never abandons His children.

The greatest gift you can offer your child isn't perfect intervention or flawless support; it's your faithful presence. Just as God assures us, "Never will I leave you; never will I forsake you" (Hebrews 13:5), your consistent love creates a sanctuary where healing can begin. Even when words fail and solutions seem out of reach, your unwavering commitment communicates a truth your child desperately needs to hear: you are worth staying for.

As you nurture your relationship through these challenges, remember that God is at work in ways you may not yet see. "Be patient, then, brothers and sisters, until the Lord's coming. See how the farmer waits for the land to yield its valuable crop, patiently waiting for the autumn and spring rains" (James 5:7). The seeds of truth, love, and faith you plant today, even in rocky soil, are tended by the Master Gardener, who nurtures growth in His perfect timing.

Hold fast to hope, even when progress seems painfully slow. "To bestow on them a crown of beauty instead of ashes, the oil of joy instead of mourning, and a garment of praise instead of a spirit of despair" (Isaiah 61:3). The God who specializes in resurrection is continually at work, bringing life from death, beauty from ashes, and joy from mourning. Your child's story, and yours, is still being written by the Author who creates the most beautiful redemption stories from our deepest struggles.

You have been chosen for this sacred work of parenting your child through this specific valley. Though the path may be difficult, you are equipped with everything you need for this journey: "His divine power has given us everything we need for a godly life through our knowledge of him who called us by his own glory and goodness" (2 Peter 1:3). Walk forward with confidence, not in your own strength, but in the unfailing love of the God who holds both you and your child in His everlasting arms.

13. Prayer Guide for Parents

The Foundation of Prayer: Repentance and Right Relationship with God

Before approaching God's throne in prayer for our children, we must first ensure our own hearts are right with Him. Scripture teaches us that repentance is essential for salvation and an ongoing right relationship with God:

"*Repent, then, and turn to God, so that your sins may be wiped out, that times of refreshing may come from the Lord.*" (Acts 3:19)

Repentance is not merely feeling sorry for sin, but a complete turning away from sin and turning toward God. It involves:

- **Acknowledgment of Sin**: "*If we claim to be without sin, we deceive ourselves and the truth is not in us.*" (1 John 1:8)
- **Godly Sorrow**: "*Godly sorrow brings repentance that leads to salvation and leaves no regret, but worldly sorrow brings death.*" (2 Corinthians 7:10)
- **Confession**: "*If we confess our sins, he is faithful and just and will forgive us our sins and purify us from all unrighteousness.*" (1 John 1:9)
- **Turning Away from Sin**: "*Let the wicked forsake their ways and the unrighteous their thoughts. Let them turn to the LORD, and he will have mercy on them, and to our God, for he will freely pardon.*" (Isaiah 55:7)
- **Bearing Fruit of Repentance**: "*Produce fruit in keeping with repentance.*" (Matthew 3:8)

As you prepare to intercede for your children, first spend time in personal repentance, allowing the Holy Spirit to search your heart and reveal any areas that require confession and cleansing. This positions you to pray from a place of spiritual authority and alignment with God's will.

"*The prayer of a righteous person is powerful and effective.*" (James 5:16)

✈ FROM THE FIELD

There were seasons in our international years when the challenges were significant enough that the only honest answer to the question of what kept us going was: we were not keeping ourselves going. God was.

What sustained us, genuinely sustained us, not as a platitude but as a lived daily reality, was the privilege of seeing God's mercy and grace at work in the lives of the people we had been called to serve. We saw people whom society had discarded find dignity and redemption in the love of Christ. We saw lives transformed in ways we could not have manufactured or explained. Those moments were not incidental to our calling. They were the fuel for it.

Prayer was not always eloquent in those years. Sometimes it was simply showing up before God with what we had, which was often not much. But it was enough. He who calls you is faithful, and He will sustain you, not necessarily in the way you expect, but in the way you need. Bring what you have. He will do the rest.

Daily Prayer Points

For Children 10-13

- **Monday:** Protection of their growing minds and hearts *"Guard their hearts and minds in Christ Jesus." (Based on Philippians 4:7)*

- **Tuesday:** Development of a personal faith beyond family tradition *"May they know you, the only true God, and Jesus Christ whom you have sent." (Based on John 17:3)*

- **Wednesday:** Healthy friendships and peer relationships *"Surround them with friends who fear your name." (Based on Psalm 119:63)*

- **Thursday:** School life and learning challenges *"Give them wisdom and understanding in all knowledge and learning." (Based on Daniel 1:17)*

- **Friday:** Preparation for adolescence *"May they increase in wisdom and stature, and in favor with God and others." (Based on Luke 2:52)*

- **Saturday:** Family relationships and sibling bonds *"Help them live in harmony with one another." (Based on Romans 12:16)*

- **Sunday:** Growing involvement in church community *"May they be planted in the house of the Lord." (Based on Psalm 92:13)*

For Teens 14-17

- **Monday:** Identity formation in Christ *"Help them understand that they are your masterpiece." (Based on Ephesians 2:10)*

- **Tuesday:** Protection in an increasingly complex world *"Keep them from the evil one." (Based on John 17:15)*

- **Wednesday:** Wisdom in relationships and social dynamics *"Grant them discernment to know who should speak into their lives." (Based on Proverbs 13:20)*

- **Thursday:** Academic pressures and future planning *"Guide their steps according to your perfect plan." (Based on Proverbs 16:9)*

- **Friday:** Emotional and mental wellbeing *"Give them your peace that passes understanding." (Based on Philippians 4:7)*

- **Saturday:** Developing spiritual disciplines *"Create in them a hunger for your Word and presence." (Based on Psalm 42:1-2)*

- **Sunday:** Involvement in youth group and Christian community *"May they not neglect meeting together with other believers." (Based on Hebrews 10:25)*

For Young Adults 18-24

- **Monday:** Clarity in vocational direction *"Make their path straight as they acknowledge you in all their ways." (Based on Proverbs 3:6)*

- **Tuesday:** Steadfastness in faith amid questioning *"Build them up in their most holy faith." (Based on Jude 1:20)*

- **Wednesday:** Wisdom in significant relationships *"Guide them to relationships that honor you." (Based on 2 Corinthians 6:14)*

- **Thursday:** Financial stewardship and independence *"Help them to be faithful with what you've entrusted to them." (Based on Matthew 25:21)*

- **Friday:** Spiritual growth and church connection *"May they be rooted and established in love." (Based on Ephesians 3:17)*

- **Saturday:** Mental and emotional health *"Heal any brokenness and bind up their wounds." (Based on Psalm 147:3)*

- **Sunday:** Kingdom impact and purpose *"Show them the good works you prepared in advance for them to do." (Based on Ephesians 2:10)*

Scripture Prayers for Repentance and Salvation

When praying specifically for your child's salvation and walk with God, use these Scripture-based prayers:

- **For Conviction of Sin**: "Holy Spirit, convict my child of sin, righteousness, and judgment. Open their eyes to see their need for a Savior." (Based on John 16:8)

- **For Genuine Repentance**: "Father, grant my child repentance leading to a knowledge of the truth, that they may come to their senses and escape the snare of the enemy." (Based on 2 Timothy 2:25-26)

- **For Salvation**: "Lord, draw my child to Jesus, for no one can come to Him unless the Father draws them. I pray they would confess with their mouth that Jesus is Lord and believe in their heart that God raised Him from the dead." (Based on John 6:44 and Romans 10:9)

- **For Spiritual Rebirth**: "Father, by Your will, bring about new birth in my child through the word of truth." (Based on James 1:18)

- **For Continued Spiritual Growth**: "Lord, help my child to put off their old self and be renewed in the spirit of their mind, putting on the new self, created after the likeness of God in true righteousness and holiness." (Based on Ephesians 4:22-24)

Scripture Prayers for Purity

Our children face unprecedented challenges to purity in today's world. These prayers address physical, mental, emotional, and spiritual purity:

- **For Pure Thoughts**: "Father, help my child to fix their thoughts on what is true, honorable, right, pure, lovely, and admirable. Help them think about things that are excellent and worthy of praise." (Based on Philippians 4:8)

- **For Sexual Purity**: "Lord, teach my child to honor You with their body as Your temple. Help them flee from sexual immorality and understand that their body is meant for the Lord, not for sexual impurity." (Based on 1 Corinthians 6:18-20)

- **For Media Discernment**: "Holy Spirit, guide my child to make wise choices about what they watch, listen to, and consume. Help them to recognize content that corrupts rather than edifies, and give them the strength to turn away from it." (Based on Psalm 101:3 and Proverbs 4:23)

- **For Pure Relationships**: "God, surround my child with friends who encourage purity and godliness. Help them to seek relationships that reflect Your love rather than worldly values." (Based on 1 Corinthians 15:33 and 2 Timothy 2:22)

- **For Heart Protection**: "Lord, guard my child's heart with all diligence, for from it flow the springs of life. May they create in themselves a clean heart through Your power." (Based on Proverbs 4:23 and Psalm 51:10)

- **For Purity Amid Temptation**: "Father, provide a way of escape when my child faces temptation. Strengthen them to honor You with their choices even when no one else is watching." (Based on 1 Corinthians 10:13)

- **For Restoration After Failure**: "God of grace, when my child falls short, help them to confess their sin and receive Your forgiveness and cleansing. Restore to them the joy of Your salvation." (Based on 1 John 1:9 and Psalm 51:12)

Scripture Prayers for Parents

Praying God's Word over your child:

- **Protection**: "Lord, be a shield around my child, their glory and the lifter of their head." (Based on Psalm 3:3)
- **Wisdom**: "Give my child a heart of wisdom to number their days." (Based on Psalm 90:12)
- **Identity**: "Help my child grasp how wide and long and high and deep is the love of Christ." (Based on Ephesians 3:18)
- **Purpose**: "Establish the work of my child's hands and fulfill Your purpose for them." (Based on Psalm 138:8)
- **Restoration**: "Restore what the locusts have eaten in my child's life." (Based on Joel 2:25)

Prayer for Parental Repentance

"Heavenly Father, I come before you acknowledging my own need for ongoing repentance. Search me, O God, and know my heart; try me and know my thoughts. See if there is any grievous way in me and lead me in the way everlasting. I confess the ways I have failed as a parent, any idols I have placed before you, any times my example has not reflected your character. Forgive me through the blood of Jesus Christ. Renew a right spirit within me. Help me to parent from a place of humility, grace, and truth, reflecting your perfect love to my children. In Jesus' name, Amen." (Based on Psalm 139:23-24)

Words of Encouragement

"Do not be anxious about anything, but in every situation, by prayer and petition, with thanksgiving, present your requests to God. And the peace of God, which transcends all understanding, will guard your hearts and your minds in Christ Jesus." (Philippians 4:6-7)
Your prayers for your child carry more power than you might realize. In those moments when words fail you, when the challenges seem too great to bear, and when you feel you've reached the limits of your own wisdom, remember that prayer opens the door to divine intervention. The time you invest in interceding for your child is never wasted, even if the answers aren't immediately visible.
God hears every whispered request, every tearful plea, and every groan of your heart. Romans 8:26-27 beautifully reassures us: "In the same way, the Spirit helps us in our weakness. We do not know what we ought to pray for, but the Spirit himself intercedes for us through wordless groans." God, who searches our hearts, knows the mind of the Spirit, as He intercedes for His people in perfect alignment with His will.
Throughout history, countless children have been carried through their darkest valleys by the faithful prayers of their parents. Your consistent spiritual support creates an invisible blanket of grace that envelops your child's journey. As Jeremiah 33:3 promises, "Call to me and I will answer you and tell you great and unsearchable things you do not know."
Don't forget that repentance opens the door to spiritual power in your prayers. 1 Peter 3:12 reminds us, "For the eyes of the Lord are on the righteous and his ears are attentive to their prayer." Walking in repentance and righteousness transforms your prayers into powerful weapons in the spiritual battle for your child's heart and mind.
Even on days when your prayers feel inadequate, trust that the Holy Spirit "intercedes for us through wordless groans" (Romans 8:26), refining your imperfect prayers into something beautiful and powerful. Keep praying, keep hoping, and keep believing, your faithful prayers hold immeasurable value in God's kingdom.

14. Conclusion: The Long View of Parenting

> "*We will not hide them from their descendants; we will tell the next generation the praiseworthy deeds of the Lord, his power, and the wonders he has done.*" (Psalm 78:4)

Embracing God's Timeline

As you journey through the challenges of parenting children and young adults in today's complex world, remember these enduring truths that can sustain you through difficult seasons:

- **God's Faithfulness Endures**: His love for your child exceeds even your own. "*Can a mother forget the baby at her breast and have no compassion on the child she has borne? Though she may forget, I will not forget you! See, I have engraved you on the palms of my hands*" (Isaiah 49:15-16).
- **Your Role Changes**: Your relationship with your child will evolve from authority to influence and wisdom as they grow, much as God relates to us first as Father but also as Friend and Counselor.
- **Seeds Take Time**: Today's guidance, prayers, and biblical foundation may bear fruit years later, sometimes after seasons of dormancy.
- **Grace Abounds**: God's grace covers both your mistakes as a parent and your child's struggles.
- **Hope Remains**: No situation, however dire, is beyond God's redemptive power. "*Behold, I am doing a new thing; now it springs forth, do you not perceive it? I will make a way in the wilderness and rivers in the desert*" (Isaiah 43:19, ESV).

The Harvest Principle

Parenting operates on God's agricultural timeline, not our immediate-results culture:

- **Sowing Faithfully**: Your consistent investment in your child's spiritual and emotional wellbeing plants seeds that may not immediately sprout. "Let us not become weary in doing good, for at the proper time we will reap a harvest if we do not give up" (Galatians 6:9).
- **Weathering Seasons**: Just as farmers endure drought, frost, and storms before harvest, parents must persevere through challenging seasons with faith.
- **Trusting the Process**: The growth happening beneath the surface, in your child's heart and mind, may not be visible to you for years.
- **Celebrating Small Growth**: Look for and affirm small evidences of character development and spiritual awareness, just as Jesus noticed faith "as small as a mustard seed."

Spiritual Legacy Beyond Crisis

Crisis moments, including mental health struggles, are chapters in your child's story, not the conclusion:

- **God's Redemptive Narrative**: Throughout Scripture, God works powerfully through people's deepest struggles, weaving them into His redemptive purposes. "*You intended to harm me, but God intended it for good to accomplish what is now being done, the saving of many lives*" (Genesis 50:20).
- **Testimony Formation**: Today's painful challenges may become tomorrow's powerful testimony of God's faithfulness.
- **Deeper Compassion**: Difficulties often cultivate deeper empathy and compassion in both parents and children. "*Praise be to the God and Father of our Lord Jesus Christ, the Father of compassion and the God of all comfort, who comforts us in all our troubles, so that we can comfort those in any trouble with the comfort we ourselves receive from God*" (2 Corinthians 1:3-4).
- **Intergenerational Impact**: Your faithful example during trials leaves a legacy beyond your child to future generations.

Extending Grace to Yourself as a Parent

As you work to support your children through challenges, remember that perfect parenting is not the goal, faithful parenting is:

- **You Will Make Mistakes**: Every parent fails, falters, and makes decisions they later regret. This is part of the human experience, not a sign of parental inadequacy.
- **Your Children Need Your Authenticity More Than Your Perfection**: When you model humility by acknowledging

mistakes, seeking forgiveness, and making amends, you teach powerful lessons about grace and growth. This authenticity is far more valuable than presenting a façade of flawless parenting.

- **God's Grace Covers Parenting Failures**: The same grace that saves us also covers our parenting shortcomings. "*But he said to me, 'My grace is sufficient for you, for my power is made perfect in weakness'*" (2 Corinthians 12:9). God can redeem and work through even our parenting missteps.

- **Self-Compassion Is Biblical**: Jesus taught us to "*love your neighbor as yourself*" (Mark 12:31), implying that appropriate self-love is the foundation for loving others well. Beating yourself up over parenting mistakes diminishes your capacity to love and guide your children effectively.

- **You're Not Parenting Alone**: God promises His presence in the parenting journey. His strength complements your weakness.

- **Today Is a New Day**: Each morning brings fresh opportunities to parent with intention. "*The steadfast love of the LORD never ceases; his mercies never come to an end; they are new every morning; great is your faithfulness*" (Lamentations 3:22-23). Yesterday's parenting mistakes don't define today's potential.

FROM THE FIELD

I carry the weight of knowing that I failed to protect my children as I should have. That is not false humility; it is simply true. But I have come to understand, through this long season of reflection and through the work of writing this resource, that God's mercy and grace are not proportional to what we deserve. I am unworthy of them. He extends them anyway.

Writing this resource has shown me every area where I wish I had done better. It has also shown me something I was not expecting: that I did some things right. At every turn where I failed, God was there helping us get through it. And because of what was poured into my children, imperfectly, inconsistently, but genuinely, they have not turned away from their faith. They have leaned into it, each of them, for themselves.

I am not the perfect father. I know that more clearly now than I ever have. But I am more open today than I have ever been, to accept what I did wrong, to sit in the grief of it without being destroyed by it, and to seek reconciliation with my children where it is still needed. That openness is not something I manufactured. It is what God has done in me through this process. If this resource does the same thing for even one parent who reads it, it will have been worth every word.

Words of Encouragement

"Now to him who is able to do immeasurably more than all we ask or imagine, according to his power that is at work within us..." (Ephesians 3:20)

Parenting is a journey measured not in days but in decades, and its true fruits often ripen long after your most active years have passed. When you find yourself feeling discouraged by current struggles or setbacks, remember: God's timeline extends far beyond what you can currently see. The prayers you've offered, the values you've modeled, the Scriptures you've shared, and the unconditional love you've shown are powerful seeds planted in fertile soil, even when that soil seems rocky or resistant.

Throughout Scripture, we see that God's most significant work often requires patient endurance through seasons of silence or struggle. Think of Abraham and Sarah, who waited decades for their promised child; Joseph, who endured years of slavery and imprisonment before seeing God's purpose fulfilled; or Moses, who spent forty years in the wilderness before leading Israel to freedom. Even David was anointed king long before he took the throne. These stories remind us that God's greatest works rarely align with our preferred timelines.

In today's challenging world, parenting requires similar patient endurance. The difficulties you encounter now are shaping in you a depth of faith, wisdom, and perseverance that casual parenting during easier times could never cultivate.

Your labor of love holds eternal significance. Even when immediate results aren't visible, trust that God is actively working through your faithful efforts, nothing done in service to Him is ever wasted.

Remember, you are part of God's own redemptive work in your child's life. The same God who pursued us with relentless love is pursuing your child. He is the God who specializes in making beauty from ashes, transforming your family's struggles into a magnificent testimony of His grace. Just as the Lord leaves the ninety-nine to find the one, He is seeking your child with tender persistence.

As you take the long view of parenting, find strength in knowing that the same God who began a good work in your child "will carry it on to completion until the day of Christ Jesus" (Philippians 1:6). Your role is essential, but it is finite; God's commitment to your child is eternal and unwavering. When your strength falters, His does not. When your wisdom reaches its limits, His is boundless. When your ability to influence seems to wane, His Spirit continues to work in ways you cannot yet see.

So stand firm in your high calling as a parent! The seeds you plant today, even when watered with tears, will be harvested with joy in God's perfect timing. Your child's story is still unfolding, and the Author of Life is writing a narrative even more beautiful and redemptive than anything you could ever craft on your own. Trust His pen, even when the current chapter feels challenging, knowing that He specializes in unexpected plot twists and glorious resolutions that display His glory and goodness.

Additional Resources

Seekers Resources

- **Seekers Parent Support Groups**: Find local groups in your area at https://iseekers.org/parents**
- **Seekers Webinars**: Monthly online training for parents at https://iseekers.org/webinars**
- **Seekers Suicide Intervention Training**: Sign-up for training at https://ssic.iseekers.org
- **Seekers Family Mentoring**: Connect with a Seekers-trained parent mentor

Seekers International Foundation resources are accessible through their website at https://iseekers.org

Christian Books and Resources

- **Faith and Parenting**
  - "Parenting: 14 Gospel Principles" by Paul David Tripp
  - "Praying the Scriptures for Your Adult Children" by Jodie Berndt
- **Mental Health Resources**
  - "Grace for the Afflicted" by Matthew S. Stanford
  - Christian counseling directory: Focus on the Family Counselor Network
- **Substance Use and Recovery**
  - "Addiction and Grace" by Gerald May
  - Celebrate Recovery program materials
- **Identity and Cultural Issues**
  - "Counter Culture" by David Platt
  - "Mama Bear Apologetics" by Hillary Morgan Ferrer

Support Communities

- **Parents in Similar Seasons**
  - Church-based parent support groups
  - Moms/Dads in Prayer groups
  - Seekers local chapters
- **Christian Counseling Options**
  - Faith-integrated family therapy
  - Church counseling ministries
  - Seekers-affiliated counseling network
- **Crisis Resources**
  - National Suicide Prevention Lifeline: 988
  - Crisis Text Line: Text HOME to 741741
  - Hope for Wholeness (faith-based support for sexual identity questions): hopeforwholeness.org

** Denotes coming soon or is in development at the time of this publication

Acknowledgments

Above all else, I am grateful to God. Every word in this resource exists because of His faithfulness, His grace, and His relentless love for families. He placed this calling on my heart, sustained me through the years it took to bring it to life, and reminded me in every difficult season that His purposes do not fail. To Him be all the glory.

To my beloved wife, who shared life with me through the years of cross-cultural ministry and our repatriation. She walked beside me through the hardest chapters of our family's story. I could not have written this without her.

To my beloved son, whose courage and resilience in the hardest of circumstances shaped my understanding of what children carry silently, and whose story is woven into the heart of this work in ways he may not yet fully know.

To my precious daughter Megan, co-founder of Steadfast Resources and the COO who helped bring this vision from manuscript to reality. Her bilingual childhood, her cross-cultural perspective, and her deep commitment to families made her an indispensable partner in every sense of the word.

To my precious youngest daughter, who taught our whole family what it looks like to absorb the world quietly, process it deeply, and emerge with a spirit that is both strong and full of grace. Her childhood gave this book its most honest pages.

To my sister Angela, whose creative gift shaped the cover of this book and whose faithful prayers and encouragement sustained me through the writing process. Her fingerprints are on this work in more ways than one.

To my daily prayer family, who interceded for this work faithfully from its earliest pages to its final ones. Their prayers, their encouragement, and their belief that this resource would reach and help families kept me moving forward on the days when the task felt too large. I am deeply grateful for every one of them.

Clinical Reviewers

This resource is stronger because of the time, expertise, and honest feedback generously offered by the following clinical professionals. Their willingness to review this manuscript before publication reflects a shared commitment to the wellbeing of families, and this work is better for their contribution.

Fernando Garzon, Psy.D.
Associate Dean and Professor, Regent University; Chair, Counseling Ministries; Licensed Psychologist

Courage Mudzongo, Ph.D.
Associate Professor, George Fox University; Certified Family Life Educator

Vickey Maclin, Psy.D.
Associate Professor in Counseling, Gordon-Conwell Theological Seminary

Kenneth A. Logan, Psy.D.
Professor of Clinical Psychology and Director of Integration, George Fox University

Legal Notices and Disclaimers

Copyright Notice

ISBN: 979-8-9963307-0-6 (Paperback)
ISBN: 979-8-9963307-1-3 (eBook)

For permission requests or inquiries about acceptable use, contact: Steadfast Resources, Ltd. Co. info@steadfastltd.io - https://steadfastltd.io

Disclaimer of Liability

The information contained in this publication is provided for educational and informational purposes only. It is not intended as and should not be relied upon as medical, psychological, legal, financial, or other professional advice.

The authors and publishers have made every effort to ensure the accuracy and completeness of information contained in this publication. However, the information is provided "as is" without warranty of any kind, either express or implied, including without limitation any implied warranties of merchantability, fitness for a particular purpose, or non-infringement.

In no event shall Steadfast Resources, Ltd. Co., its authors, contributors, or the publisher be liable for any direct, indirect, incidental, special, exemplary, punitive, or consequential damages whatsoever resulting from the use of this publication, even if advised of the possibility of such damage.

Medical/Mental Health Disclaimer

This book is not intended to replace professional medical or mental health advice, diagnosis, or treatment. Always seek the advice of your physician, mental health professional, or other qualified health provider with any questions you may have regarding a medical or mental health condition. Never disregard professional medical or mental health advice or delay in seeking it because of something you have read in this publication.

If you or someone you know is experiencing a medical or mental health emergency, including but not limited to thoughts of suicide or self-harm, please call 988 (National Suicide Prevention Lifeline), dial 911, or go to your nearest emergency room immediately.

Religious Content Notice

This publication contains religious content based on Christian beliefs and scriptural references. The views, interpretations, and applications of scripture expressed herein represent the understanding of Steadfast Resources, Ltd. Co. but may differ from those held by other religious organizations or individuals.

Trademark Notice

All product names, logos, brands, trademarks, and registered trademarks mentioned in this publication are the property of their respective owners. All company, product, and service names used in this publication are for identification purposes only. Use of these names, trademarks, and brands does not imply endorsement.

Privacy Policy

For information about how Steadfast Resources, Ltd. Co. collects, uses, and protects personal information, please refer to our Privacy Policy, available at https://steadfastltd.io/privacy-policy-2.

Bible Version Notice

First Edition Notice

First Edition: 2026 Printed in the United States of America

www.ingramcontent.com/pod-product-compliance
Lightning Source LLC
LaVergne TN
LVHW090515110826
845146LV00003B/868

* 9 7 9 8 9 9 6 3 3 0 7 0 6 *